Going Deep:

Taking Children into the Spiritual Depths with God

Clint May

L.I.T. MINISTRIES
Empowering The **Next Generation**

GOING DEEP: TAKING CHILDREN INTO THE SPIRITUAL DEPTHS WITH GOD

Published by
L.I.T. Ministries
P.O. Box 186
Weatherford, TX 76086

Written by Dr. Clint May, President, L.I.T. Ministries
Edited by Amy McMullin
Book layout design by Rachel Jackson

diverse envisions
creative design

ENDORSEMENTS

I was deeply moved as I read about the journey God has brought Dr. Clint May through. I can see that God has led us to him and his ministry for such a time as this!

In 2009, I had a vision where God showed me an endless sea of African children, and He simply said, "Reach them." That led us to launch "Vision 2020 — Reaching 1,000,000 children in Burkina." We accomplished that mission in 2020 by sending teams with puppets and skits throughout Burkina. But as soon as we finished, we knew that there was something missing. We knew we needed to train the church to disciple these children.

So, we started looking for curriculum that we could provide to our volunteers. We SCOURED the internet, talked to churches, looked at all the popular curriculum that's out there. They all taught Bible stories and gave moral lessons, but none of them DISCIPLED!

I had a conviction that children were capable of so much more than what the church expected, but I didn't know how to get there. Reading this book and knowing Clint's story has deeply inspired me. I am excited to take this to Burkina and see this nation transformed as the next generation is MOBILIZED and empowered to become the missional force that God intends for them to be!

I sincerely believe that "Child Evangelism, Discipleship, and Mobilization" is God's preeminent strategy to finish the Great Commission. I love that Clint humbly stumbled his way into this God-strategy, simply obeying God's next command. I know that He will continue to open bigger doors of opportunity for Clint and his ministry!

As a child evangelist and a 20-year missionary, I have trained teams in Africa that have shared the Gospel with more than a million children, with hundreds of thousands coming to salvation. But I have always had the nagging question: "What happens after we leave? Are the children we are reaching being discipled?" I felt that the children were capable of so much more than just attending church.

GOING DEEP was equal parts deeply convicting and encouraging— challenging me that we need to lead children past the salvation experience to the fullness of purpose for which God has designed each one of them. The stories that Clint shares undeniably and vividly demonstrate the power of mobilizing children as agents of the Great Commission. Children are not meant to be idle bystanders; they do not have a "Junior Holy Spirit."

We have always believed that children can be saved. What GOING DEEP shows through the captivating stories and experiences Clint has gathered over decades of ministry, is that children can become powerful agents of the Gospel if they are challenged to live out their faith and given opportunities to step out in faith.

I am excited to get this book into the hands of church leaders. If they are half as inspired as I am, this book will revolutionize their ministry to children!

—JOEL HAYSLIP, Regional Director,
West and Central Africa,
Go To Nations;
Manager, Field Ministry and Discipleship (UPG & Ministry Partner),
Samaritan's Purse I OPERATION CHRISTMAS CHILD

The coming generations are filled with passionate, committed, and driven leaders. Not leaders just for the future, but for right here and now. Years ago, I was interviewing a young leader at a conference, and I asked her what we could do as more seasoned leaders to support her and her generation. She told me that I was doing what they needed: listening and giving them a voice. That is what Clint May does in this book. Through countless stories and statements from young leaders themselves, he presents a compelling vision of what God can do and is indeed doing through this generation. You will be encouraged, and you will be challenged. Thank you for writing this book, Clint, so that the voices of these incredible leaders may be heard.

— **THOMAS HARLEY, Vice President, OneHope**

Clint May has been a champion for kids and an innovator for many years. In this book, he offers a huge piece of the puzzle of not just reaching a generation but releasing them into the fullness of God's call on their lives. He is on the cutting edge of what it means to empower kids by equipping and making space for them to have their own God stories. In this book, you will be inspired and challenged by real-life stories of what kids can do if given an opportunity. I agree with Clint that God is raising up a generation to change the world and their time is NOW!

— **RICK OLMSTEAD, Executive Director, Global 4/14 Window Movement; President, Generation Now**

In 2002, Christ began to reveal something to Clint May that has transformed his life and the lives of preteens and ministry leaders around the world: the power of equipping children and preteens for ministry. In these pages, you'll read the story of how the Holy Spirit awakened a passion in Clint and how that flicker of revelation has become a contagious fire that continues to impact preteens as it spreads far beyond what Clint ever imagined. You'll be inspired by stories of how God speaks to and empowers kids for powerful ministry of their own, and you'll find yourself asking God to equip you to train up the next generation to share the Gospel and grow the Kingdom.

— SEAN SWEET, Preteen Pastor, Destiny Church in Rocklin, CA; Author of Let Go and Run Beside: Essentials of Intentional Preteen Ministry

C. S. Lewis popularized the argument that Jesus was either a liar, a lunatic, or Lord. I believe Jesus demonstrated clearly that He was not only Lord, but the Lord over all of humanity. Dr. Clint May takes readers on a journey in his new book, GOING DEEP: TAKING CHILDREN INTO THE SPIRITUAL DEPTHS WITH GOD, a journey experienced by him and many of his colleagues. Thank you for putting into print how Jesus is changing the world through the obedience of children.

— JACK TERRELL, Founder and President, KiDs Beach Club®

Can children talk to Jesus? Can children walk with Jesus? Indeed, they can! Clint May is on mission to help us all rethink the role children play in church. Every person involved in working with kids needs to read this book.

— JACK D. EGGAR, President, Global Children's Network

In 2009, the 4 to 14 Window Movement began. The goal was to Awaken the Church around the world to the priority of children ages 4 to 14, to Reach them as the most responsive to the Gospel, to Rescue those who were exploited, to Root them through discipleship, and to Release them as Full Partners in God's Mission. I met Clint May as we began to journey together in this movement. He was ahead of most of us because God had been teaching him for many years earlier that there is "no Junior Holy Spirit!" We've become convinced that the 2+ billion children in the world under age 15 are the "great untapped harvest force." If you haven't yet discovered this amazing truth, you are in for a wonderful surprise. GOING DEEP tells Clint's story—or really God's story. It's a story that has the potential to change your life. I encourage you to read it for yourself.

— **TOM VICTOR, President, The Great Commission Coalition; Member, Global Children's Task Force**

I have been a witness to the stories and principles found in GOING DEEP and will forever be grateful for how these principles have impacted my family and ministry. You will read stories of how kids CAN be the Church. You will hear of stories that can only be credited to the Holy Spirit. You will read stories of spiritual giants in the form of kids who simply said yes to Jesus.

It was more than ten years ago when as a Families Pastor I was searching for the missing piece of discipleship with kids and I was introduced to Leaders In Training. It literally changed my life as a father in discipling my kids and as a pastor in raising up kids and students to BE the Church.

In GOING DEEP, you will be introduced to the same principles as I was years ago, and my prayer is that you will take hold of the reality that God CAN use kids to advance the Gospel and make disciples. You will be challenged as I was to think differently and believe that kids can be the Church.

— **MIKE LEHEW, Executive Director, Mobile Missions Network**

I wholeheartedly agree with Clint May's philosophy and practice of Children's Ministry. Our ministry is not just TO children...it is WITH children. Walking alongside them, giving them the tools and the confidence to discover and develop the gifts that God has given them at the time of their salvation, however young that may be. They are our brothers and sisters in Christ, and we are to carry the Gospel to this broken world WITH THEM! I pray the stories of how these children are boldly reaching our world for Christ will inspire you to 'go deep' with God and with His children!

— JERRY LAWRENCE, Adjunct Professor of Educational Ministries & Leadership and DEdMin Children's Ministry Cohort; Alumni & Career Services Counselor, Dallas Theological Seminary

With painter's tape and a passion that is rare, Dr. Clint May lays out a highly effective method of leadership training for the "now generation!" Through active, hands-on leadership involvement, Clint will cause you to rethink how you look at your children and your children's ministry. Trust me, this works! I have implemented the Ephesians 4 principles taught in this book—you will never have a shortage of leaders ever again. You will be inspired by the testimonies from children being seen, rather than "targets of ministry" to being treated, as "teammates in ministry!"

— PASTOR D.J. BOSLER, GameLife123: Children Focused Church Planting

TABLE OF CONTENTS

FOREWORD

I am a member of Wedgwood Baptist Church in Fort Worth. In 2002, our church called Clint May as Children's Pastor. Even though he had been in children's ministry for years, he was not content with business as usual. He began to think new thoughts about genuinely discipling children and then mobilizing them for the Great Commission.

As Clint began making those changes that would later be named Nehemiah Kids and Leaders In Training, I had a front-row seat. Because his vision for children was similar to my vision for teenagers, we were drawn toward each other. Soon, we began sharing meals. Over the years, the number of barbecue meals we have shared will probably shorten our lives.

Soon, I saw children being genuinely discipled in ways that reminded me of solid student ministries. Predictably, children began reading and memorizing the Bible on their own. They began praying with more depth and passion.

Then, I saw children being trained and equipped so they could pursue the Great Commission. But Clint was not content to see children equipped for the future only. Remarkably, he had the vision to send out preteen missionaries today.

I was amazed to see preteens leading (not assisting with, but leading) evangelistic Bible studies, clubs, block parties, and outreaches locally. Success there led to trips for that same purpose in the state. Success there led to trips out of state. Children leading children to Jesus blew me away. I observed children speaking and leading worship music on stage. Children were teaching the Bible studies, crafts, and recreation. Children were weeping for lost people who were attending their outreaches.

I thought only older teenagers could do these things. But they were being done with quality and kingdom impact by 10-year-olds!

You cannot keep something that remarkable a secret. Other church leaders who were pursuing the Great Commission began to hear about preteen disciples in our church. Soon, a new way of seeing children's ministry spilled out of our church and became a movement. Today, scores of churches embrace the DNA and resources of L.I.T.

I know Clint May. He adores King Jesus, and he is rock solid theologically. He draws everything he writes and develops from the proper exegesis of Scripture. His character is sterling. His commitment to the harvest is unwavering. In short, I trust him to lead the Church into new ways of ministering to, with, and through children.

Clint says, "Our mandate is the Great Commission, and [children] are to be included as co-equals in His commission." That is the primary thesis of the entire book.

Is the Great Commission a mandate for the believer in a nursing home? Yes. Is the Great Commission a mandate for a 4th grader? Yes. Do both have strengths and challenges? Yes. But from the moment of redemption to the moment of death, the Great Commission is a mandate for every believer every day.

The Church does not disciple and equip preteens so they can accelerate the harvest someday.

The Church disciples and equips them so they can be part of the harvest today.

While on a L.I.T. mission trip, a children's minister reported, "This is the first time I have had children under my leadership lead someone to the Lord. I am overwhelmed and blown away by how God can use our kids. It's amazing to me."

Children's pastors, volunteers, and parents all need to consider:

- Do we believe children receive the Holy Spirit at the time of their salvation?

- Do we believe that the Holy Spirit is active and alive in them from day one?

- Do we believe children receive spiritual gifts at the time of their salvation?

- Do we believe the Spirit can work through children's gifts to introduce people to Jesus?

Why are so few adult believers actively involved in Great Commission activity? Why do so few take the Gospel outside the church? The following lines provide much of the answer:

Children:
"We just met Jesus. He is wonderful. Now we want to do something for Him."

Leaders:
"Later. Right now, just sit still and listen."

Teenagers:
"We love Jesus. He is wonderful. Now we want to do something for Him."

Leaders:
"Later. Right now, just sit still and listen."

Leaders:
"Adults, why do you just sit? Get up and do something for Jesus."

Adults:
"No. We will continue to sit, just as you trained us to do for 18 years."

A church leader observed children during a L.I.T. mission trip. He provided a report about one of the children: "Shelley taught and then gave an invitation and asked those who wanted to trust Christ to raise their hands. A mother, daughter, and granddaughter all raised their hands. Shelley sat down on the curb with them and led three generations to Christ today."

That is precisely why I believe so much in the message of this book. Read every line closely.

DR. RICHARD ROSS
PhD, Senior Professor of Student Ministry,
Southwestern Seminary in Fort Worth, TX
www.RichardARoss.com

INTRODUCTION

My greatest joy throughout the past 33 years has been working with children in the local church. I have loved seeing their lives transformed by the power of the Gospel working in them. What I did not know was God's greater plan for their lives.

During my first 14 years of ministry, I was working at an adult level. Pouring my life into my adult leaders and equipping them for works of ministry (Ephesians 4:11-13). I knew that if I spent time with them, it would pour over into the lives of the children of my church. It did, and it did not.

For years I had a wrong perception of a child. They were to be seen and not heard. I saw them as the target of my ministry. I passionately tried everything I could do to reach them with the Gospel and bring them into the Church.

I am a child evangelist at heart, so that came easy to me. But something was wrong with this picture. After reaching them, I sat them down and told them how to live for Jesus. Never did I allow them to join me in ministry or even consider it. They were spectators in a game that they would not be able to play until they were much older.

Unexpectedly, my eyes were opened to something altogether different from what I had always been taught. It was as if a veil had been removed from my eyes. Now I saw children as younger brothers and sisters in Christ—the Church now.

The Lord revealed to me that children receive everything they need to be a part of the Church at the new birth. They are born again, sealed by the Holy Spirit, gifted by the Holy Spirit, empowered by the Holy Spirit, and so much more.

My purpose for writing this book is to invite you on this journey. I want to tell you my story and the stories of others to encourage and spark a fire and passion in you for the kids in your church. I want us to look at Scripture together to see that what we are witnessing is backed up by the Word of God. I will be giving you some ideas to help you begin this incredible ride in your own church as well. Hang on as we start this magnificent journey together.

DR. CLINT MAY
President, L.I.T. Ministries
www.LeadersInTraining.com

CHAPTER 1

Moving Beyond the Ministry Box

Have you ever woken up in the middle of the night and felt like God was speaking to you? As I lay in bed one night, the Lord began to remind me of stories of how He has moved in and through children, preteens, and students that I have had the privilege of ministering with through the years.

God flooded my thoughts with many beautiful stories and testimonies for the next three hours. Those stories continue to linger in my mind. God is working powerfully in the lives of children today. He is moving in ways you might never imagine, and this is happening all around the world.

I want to clarify up front by giving glory to the Lord, as the stories are of Him and His work, not mine. Sometimes, I get off track and begin to think that I am all that, but the Lord reminds me over and over again that this ministry is His—not mine. I am much like Paul, who said, "I am the worst of sinners," yet somehow God chose me and has allowed me to be a part of His plan and purpose.

You see, my journey in children's ministry began more than 33 years ago. I started attending seminary in January 1989. At the time, I knew the Lord had called me there, that it was His will for my life. However, I was not sure what His plans were; I just knew I was supposed to be there.

After about three months in seminary, my wife met a pastor's wife from a church in Cleburne, Texas. She invited us to visit their church, so we met up with them the following Sunday. It was a small church with only about 50 people. It did not particularly make an impression on me; I did not feel anything special about it.

The next evening, the pastor stopped by our house to visit. He asked me directly, "Clint, would you pray about being our children's minister?" I was thinking in my heart, "No way!" We continued to visit throughout the next three months. We loved the people, and we would go up on the weekend and help with projects at the church. But we made no commitment...yet.

I began helping with the children's church, and I truly loved it. It was not long before I knew that I was in the right place and that God was calling me to work with children. When I started, I had no earthly idea what I was doing, but through the grace of God and a lot of prayers, the Lord worked in my life and ministry in wonderful ways.

When summer arrived, I attended my first children's camp. I was so filled with joy as I walked around the camp with the kids from my church. During the last day of camp as I was listening to the children worshipping the Lord, tears rolled down my face. It was at that moment that I knew without a doubt that I was in the middle of God's will, and I loved it. I have now served on staff at five churches as a children's pastor.

Preteen L.I.T. (Leaders In Training)

At the beginning of the summer in 2002, I accepted a new children's ministry position at Wedgwood Baptist Church in Fort Worth, Texas. Right from the start, the Lord quickly moved me out of my ministry box into a new paradigm. The Lord began to lead me down a new path to train and equip preteens in my church for ministry. He turned my whole life and ministry upside down because of what I witnessed. We called this new preteen ministry L.I.T. (Leaders In Training).

That first summer, we taught preteens how to share their faith, and then we took them outside the church to minister. We did what is often called a backyard Bible club. At the time, I allowed the kids to do everything except teach the Bible studies. We trained them to minister with puppets, lead worship, and run our sound system. Our plan was for them to do everything.

As we moved through the week of our Bible club, I watched the excitement in the preteens rise as they ministered to the children that attended. On Wednesday, I taught the Bible study and gave an invitation for children to respond to the Gospel. Three children raised their hands and wanted to talk with someone about accepting Christ. This was exactly what we were there to do.

I asked three of our preteens to counsel the children that came forward. They took the children aside, sat down with them, and started talking with them about the Gospel. They read through the Counseling Card we had provided for them, and then, one-by-one, the preteens bowed their heads and prayed with the children they had counseled.

I had my doubts and was unsure if the preteens really could have done it. However, when I sat down and spoke with the three children that had been counseled by the preteens, I was convinced they had made genuine professions of faith in Christ.

In His still, small voice, the Lord asked me a question: "Clint, is the abundant life I give for children, too? Or is it just for youth and adults?" The answer I found in the days to come was—YES, it is for children, too! He has a wonderful plan for them to be the Church today—now.

That summer I also taught children how to walk with Christ daily. We taught them:

- To be in the Word of God daily
- The importance of memorizing Scripture
- That Christ must be Lord each day of our lives
- To faithfully share their faith with others
- To serve in the church

That summer of 2002, we began to see transformation in the lives of preteens right before our eyes. They were different because they had learned to sit at the feet of the Master. They were on fire about their faith, and they felt like they were a part of the church because they served alongside adults in ministry.

My First Preteen Mission Trip

In the spring of 2004, I felt led by the Lord to train and prepare the preteens for our first mission trip. We taught them to lead the worship songs, teach an evangelistic Bible study, and counsel lost children. When I shared with my church staff what I was going to do that summer, they thought I had lost my mind.

The time for our mission trip arrived, and we loaded up 27 preteens and 10 adults and headed to Corpus Christi, Texas, a drive that was a little more than 6 hours away. We planned to let our preteens lead the Bible studies in three apartment complexes for five days. As we drove down from Fort Worth, I found myself asking, "Lord, did I hear you right?" I questioned my decision to do this. Even some adults who went on the trip had difficulty letting the kids do everything.

On Monday of the mission trip, we sent three groups of preteens and leaders into the apartments to minister. At one location, an 11-year-old preteen named Mark stood up to teach. When he wrapped up his message that day, he gave an invitation for the children to respond to the Gospel. Seven kids came forward to make a decision—four children and three teenagers. The adult leaders there were shocked by what they had witnessed.

Later that afternoon, Mark approached me and asked if he could talk with me. I said, "Sure!" He said, "Brother Clint, when I was speaking today, I felt something like fire going through me." Wow! I had never heard anything like this from an adult before, much less a child. I told Mark, "That was the Holy Spirit speaking through you—Acts 1:8!"

After that first summer, I began videotaping and documenting what we were witnessing. I honestly had never seen anything like this in my previous years of ministry, and I felt like it was a marvelous move of God. These videos and stories have opened the eyes and hearts of many leaders in the Church today.

Some time ago, I woke up in the middle of the night, and this passage of Scripture came to my mind: "Do not remember the former things, Nor consider the things of old. Behold, I will do a new thing, Now it shall spring forth; Shall you not know?" (Isaiah 43:18-19). I, like many leaders, have never witnessed anything like this, and we are blessed and amazed by this powerful work of God.

Growing up in a church that took children out on mission, Channing Buchanan Haye (L.I.T. 2006-2007) commented,

> I don't think it occurred to me, until much later, that not all 5th and 6th graders had the same experiences at their churches that

we did. Even at such a young age, we were able to build true community with one another with Jesus as the foundation. We got to come together with like-minded believers and GO, like we are commanded, to teach about Christ and the Good News.

The Cross

In the spring of 2005, I had a strange dream one evening. It was so different to me that I wrote it down. Here is what I remember: I was walking through a building with my friend Jeff. It was a vast, vacant building, and as we walked toward the back, we turned a corner and went into a small room. There in the room was a black chalkboard on the wall.

Jeff asked me, "Clint, what does God want for kids today?" I walked over to the chalkboard and picked up a piece of white chalk to write out what was on my mind. Jeff stopped me. He said, "Wait a minute!" Then he reached into a bag he was carrying and pulled out a piece of yellow chalk. He said, "Here you go. Use this!"

I took the yellow chalk from him and drew a cross on the board. I remember writing out the following words and feeling compelled to explain the meaning to Jeff:

- **Lordship**—lead them to abandon all to follow Christ

- **Prayer**—model for them how to intercede for others and engage in spiritual warfare

- **Bible study**—be dedicated to the exposition of the Word of God to study and teach it

- **Evangelism**—set them on a mission to reach the lost by creating a missions mindset as the norm

- **Gifts and service**—help them discover their spiritual gifts and be determined to do our best to help them use their gifts for Him, to focus on using them to build up His Church and expand His kingdom

- **Life of Obedience**—move them from understanding Scripture to applying it, obeying God's Word, and experiencing changed lives

About three months later, we were on our way to Houston, Texas, with 50 preteens and leaders for our second preteen mission trip. Before the trip, I felt led by the Lord to call our preteens to surrender their lives fully to Him. While our preteens and leaders visited the ministry sites on Sunday afternoon, I set up at the host church for our worship time.

To prepare for worship, I moved all the chairs out of the middle of the room and stacked them up against the walls. Next, I took a roll of painter's tape and laid out a massive block cross on the floor. After putting down the tape, I reset the chairs in the room as normal. The room was ready for our worship time that evening. Needless to say, I had no idea what was coming that night.

As the preteens sang, they poured out their hearts to the Lord in worship. They were excited and, at the same time, fearful about the next day when they would go out and share Christ. As our worship service progressed, it came time for my message. I read the following passages of Scripture to them:

- **Luke 9:23**—"If anyone desires to come after Me, let him deny himself, and take up his cross daily, and follow Me."

- **Romans 12:1**—"I beseech you therefore, brethren, by the mercies of God, that you present your bodies a living sacrifice, holy, acceptable to God, which is your reasonable service."

The kids were listening as I shared: "Guys, Jesus calls us to lay down our lives in total surrender to Him. When we lay down our lives, we experience all God has planned for us. We experience the abundant life that He promises to all who follow Him (John 10:10)." I explained further the cost of following Christ and that it is a call to follow Him in obedience.

As we came to the time of invitation, I asked the children to stand up and move their chairs quietly to the sides of the room. Then I directed them to stand around the outside of the cross that was laid out on the floor. I said, "We are going to play the song The Wonderful Cross (by Chris Tomlin). If you are serious about giving your life fully to Christ and surrendering to Him, here is your invitation.

"When you hear the words, 'Oh the wonderful cross bids me come and die that I might truly live,' step into the cross if you are ready." The song began to play, and the kids stood around the room with their heads down, looking at the cross on the floor. When they heard the words of the song, "...bids me come and die that I might truly live," they all stepped into the cross, including all of the adults. It was a beautiful, holy moment watching them take this step of faith.

When the music stopped playing, we felt God's presence fall powerfully on us. We felt such a strong manifestation of the Spirit of God in the room, it was indescribable. God broke our preteens and adults over sin in their lives. They were making their hearts right before the Lord, many in tears and weeping.

They stayed in the cross for several hours, praying and praying for each other. They naturally moved into circles and prayed in groups, and I saw them lay their hands on each other and pray specifically for those in their groups.

As the kids went about their activities the following day, they were different. God had done a new work in them. They became fearless in sharing their faith. There was a new excitement that was evident all around. These children had been touched in a powerful way by the Spirit of God.

Some leaders questioned what had happened. They were just kids, and this was an emotional thing—it was not real. The following evening, the Lord showed up again. We heard them weeping and crying, which quickly progressed to sobbing again. It became apparent they were crying out to God for their lost family members. They were so deeply burdened that they could not stop crying.

During the week, we saw the children move from being shy preteens to fearless followers of Christ. The kids were witnessing to everyone they encountered there. The doubts that many of the adults on the trip were having soon moved to astonishment as we saw the Holy Spirit working in and through the preteens.

On Thursday evening of the trip, I invited the kids and leaders to testify. I wanted them to share what the Lord was doing in their lives this week.

As they began telling their stories, many of the leaders would break into tears. Their stories did not sound like something you would hear from children. Leaders said that the preteens seemed to be speaking on an adult level even though they were kids.

One young man stood up and said, "God has told me that one day I will speak for Him before thousands of people." Another shared, "I feel that God is calling me to be a missionary." Still, another young man confessed, "God has shown me that I must die to myself daily and allow Him to live through me."

I went to bed that evening feeling completely wiped out. In the middle of the night, I found myself pondering the past week. Then I remembered my dream. I thought about the yellow chalk, and I asked the Lord what it meant. In His still, small voice, I heard, "It is My glory."

Here is what we witnessed that week that transpired from my dream:

- **Lordship**—We witnessed children surrender their lives to Christ. They were broken over sin and became sold out for Him.

- **Prayer**—They became intercessors and prayer warriors. They came boldly to the throne of grace.

- **God's Word**—The Word of God came alive to them as they heard it, proclaimed it, and lived it out.

- **Evangelism**—They became fearless in sharing the Gospel and firm in their mission.

- **Gifts and ministry**—Their spiritual gifts manifested before our eyes as they taught and ministered together. They became teachers, evangelists, encouragers, leaders, shepherds, and more.

- **Obedience**—They walked away committed to faithfully living in obedience to Christ.

On Friday evening of the week, we invited the children and their families to an evening event that we called Kids Blitz: Kids Reaching Kids. We sang the songs from the Bible study sites, and we had puppet skits and drama skits. It was a fun night, and our preteens were on fire leading the time of worship and sharing Christ.

Then it came time for a presentation of the Gospel. One of our preteens, Trent (12 years old), had prepared to share the Gospel message using the Wordless Book. Before he went up on stage, he came to me and said, "Brother Clint, I am really scared." I asked him, "Trent, what do you need to do?" He said, "Surrender."

Minutes later, he walked up on the platform in front of about 185 people that night. Trent started out feeling extremely nervous, but then the Holy Spirit took over and spoke through him. There was a boldness in his voice that astonished me.

Father, thank You for letting all these kids come here tonight. And I pray that while they sit here, You will listen and that You will touch their hearts with Your Word. And I pray that You would give me Your words to speak so that they may truly know that You are Lord. Amen.

Hi. I'm Trent. And I have with me today the Wordless Book. This has no words, just color, okay? So, I am going to start at the end instead of the beginning. This gold page stands for Heaven. Everything in Heaven is gonna be gold. It's gonna be perfect. Jesus said, "I go to prepare a place for you." But we can't get to Heaven because we have sin in our lives.

(At this point, the fear left him, and you could see a new confidence come over Trent.)

Sin is anything you think, say, or do that displeases God. In Romans 3:23, it says, "All have sinned and fallen short of the glory of God." In Romans 6:23, it says, "For the wages of sin is death, but the free gift of God is eternal life through Christ Jesus our Lord." The red page represents Jesus' blood shed on the cross for you. Jesus died for your sins. He didn't die for His sins because He had no sins. He died for your sins. In John 3:16, it says, "For God so loved the world..."

(Right then, the lights dropped out in the building and then came back on again. Also, the CD in the player started playing. It did not even cause Trent to miss a beat.)

"...that He gave His only begotten Son, that whosoever believes in Him should not perish but have eternal life." God sent His Son for you. He sent His Son to die for you. Next is the white page. This represents that we need to choose to receive Him, choose to receive Him as your Savior and Lord. So, it's as easy as ABC. A, admit that you are a sinner. B, believe that Jesus is God's Son and that He died for you on the cross for your sins. And C, choose to receive Him. I would like everybody to close your eyes and bow your heads, please. I'm gonna pray for you. And then, if you would like to receive Christ as your Lord, I would like you to raise your hand after the prayer, okay? Father, thank You for this wonderful day, and I pray that this message has touched their hearts, and that they may see You. In Your name, Amen. Okay, heads bowed and eyes closed still, please. Okay, if you would like to receive God as your personal Savior and Lord and ask Him to come into your heart and save you from your sin, please raise your hand right now.

(At that moment, hands popped up all across the auditorium.)

Trent concluded, *If you raised your hand, would you walk over here? We have some people who want to talk to you.*

Many children and some adults in the room moved to the front of the room and sat down with preteens who counseled them.

I saw Trent shortly afterward, and he was relieved. I asked him how he felt about his message. He said, "I don't remember a word I just said." I was thinking, "Wow! He does not remember a word he said, and he just spoke powerfully for the Lord." In the chapters to come, I will share many more similar stories.

When we returned home, it was hard for others to understand what we had witnessed. However, even today, all those who attended this trip remember how the Lord moved in powerful ways. This trip truly changed our lives in so many ways.

As the Lord moved me in this new ministry direction, I began to hear stories from around the world. God was using children in powerful ways in other countries in ways that you would never imagine. It confirmed to me that what we were seeing in our church was happening around the world as well.

At the time, Christian leaders internationally were beginning to recognize the value of children in the Church and became committed to rallying the Church worldwide to reach them. The movement, called the 4/14 Window Movement, asserts that 70 percent of those who trust Christ worldwide do so between the ages of 4 and 14 years.[1]

In 2013, I attended the 4/14 Window Global Summit in Bangkok, Thailand. On the first evening of the event, one of the leaders shared that more than 900 Christian leaders from 97 countries were in attendance. During the conference, Dr. Luis Bush shared something that I will never forget:

> There is a call going out to champion a climb to a new mountain. A mountain that is the rooting and releasing of this new generation of world changers from the 4 to 14 Window. We believe that children and youth are not just objects of our mission, but they are also ready as anointed and appointed by God through the Spirit to be our partners strategically in His mission to the world. The urgency of this hour is the issues of rooting them in the Word of God and the purpose of God and raising them up to be His instruments, not as adjuncts in the mission of God, but His agents in the mission of God.[2]

This charge has become my mission in life. I pray that Christian leaders around the world would make it their mission in life as well. God has a plan for children and students in the Church. We must come together as the body of Christ to reach them, disciple them, equip them, and release them to minister within the church and as missionaries in the world today. It is time to stand in the gap for this young generation of believers.

As I began this new direction in 2002, I fell in love with an age group called preteens, or tweens. They were so open and excited about their faith. They had questions, but they were so pliable to God's plan for their lives. They wanted to serve, and they did it in the power of the Spirit of God living in them. To this day, they are one of my all-time favorite age groups.

After witnessing this for several years in the lives of our preteens, I saw many of the same things happening in the lives of younger children in my church. The Lord wanted this for them as well; they were not too young for the Holy Spirit to move in and through their lives. They, too, were ready and willing to serve alongside us.

At one point, my eyes were opened to the great value of our students in our church. I did not have to lose the opportunity to pour into them when they moved up into the youth group. I found ways to continue to invest in their lives and give them opportunities to minister and serve within the children's ministry. They became terrific leaders. In time, a number of them led out and directed quite a few of the 30 mission trips we have been on together.

The Impact of "The Wonderful Cross" *by Alex Burnett (L.I.T. 2004-2005)*

Church attendance was part of being in my family. On Wednesdays, we would go to whatever age-appropriate ministry was being put on. It was in L.I.T. where I learned what it meant to take the gifts and talents God had given and use them for the sake of sharing the Gospel and sharing the opportunity of life following after Jesus. Even if it was just behind a curtain making a felt likeness (puppet) lip sync the words to "Shine" (by Newsboys), I felt as though I was part of something—a team of people committed to each other and something of purpose. The leaders cared for us as kids, as Christian brothers and sisters, and as individuals with troubles never too trivial to attend to and worries worth their time.

For this homesick and anxiety-ridden 6th grader, who much preferred homeschooling to the bullies in public school, a short time in south Texas sharing the Gospel with a book of colors, a puppet show, and generally, a bunch of fun people my age and leaders who were safe to be around became a life-altering moment in my walk with Christ. I still remember the night...the emotions and the call for repentance. We would spend time with the Lord. Entering into a room with a large white tape outline of a cross, we gathered around the edges of the room. I happened to find myself standing just on the edge of the line. "When you're ready to lay down all the wrong things in your life, all the worries, your whole life, I want you to take a step into the cross." In my heart I heard, "Everything that holds you back, I can take for you—it's not yours to bear. The rejections, the loneliness, the fears, the anxieties, the anger in your heart—I can take it all. You can have My peace, My grace. And the life that you preach to others, you can live in fully."

I can remember that, without a band, track 3 on the CD, Chris Tomlin's take on "Oh the wonderful Cross" started to play, and I stepped over the line. Like the ceiling fell on me, I fell to my knees, and overwhelmed by a sensation of being known and being loved, I gave it all up—everything to Jesus. I stayed there for a while, many of us beginning to put arms around each other, and we prayed simple prayers of dedication to God and to each other.

And the lonely 6th grader who struggled to leave home for more than a night would one day fly 5,000 miles away as a missionary to the UK and later become an elder at a church in Colorado. Those years with L.I.T. were my first encounters with missions, and they were when my heart warmed to going out and sharing the Gospel, or good news, baptizing them, and training in the ways of Jesus. I'll be forever grateful.

CHAPTER 2

Understanding God's Divine Plan and Purpose for Children and Students Today

In 2006, other churches began to inquire about our preteen ministry. We shared our discipleship resources with them and invited them to join us on our preteen mission trips. During a mission trip in 2015, I took some time to interview adult leaders who served with the kids. Marc was a leader and a father to one of the children on the trip. He shared what he witnessed that week: "We have seen kids this week grow rapidly beyond their abilities. They performed at a depth of sharing the Gospel with other kids beyond what we know they could normally do. I am a 6th grade teacher, and I know their level of maturity and where they are.

1. We have seen them go beyond that rapidly here, which could only be God working in their lives.

2. We have also seen the working of the Holy Spirit. We have seen God's work and the Holy Spirit's work, and it has been real.

3. We have seen Him break them over sins in their lives, and then it makes them want to be more outgoing with the Gospel.

4. We have also seen them take on a kind of a heart for kids in this community. You would not expect that. They are not from here. They are from all over the place. They care about the kids they have met.

5. They pray for them...beyond what you would normally see with a bunch of kids this age."

Marc witnessed firsthand the same scenario many have seen on our mission trips with preteens and students. At first from their perspective, they might believe their kids are not ready or mature enough. That concern is dissolved very quickly when the Spirit of God moves in and through their lives. Then there is no doubt that the Spirit is at work in children, and it has nothing to do with personal maturity but their willingness to be used by God.

Channing Haye (former L.I.T.) shared, "The importance of being ready to share your testimony as well as the Good News at any moment with anyone is something that I experienced in L.I.T. and have carried through to my adult life."

God has a plan and a calling for children today. This chapter will look at Scripture and what it says about a believing child. God has a purpose for them now. It is incredible to witness the Holy Spirit drawing them to Himself. As they trust Christ, they have a divine calling today that He has for them to fulfill.

A. Salvation

"For God so loved the world that He gave His only begotten Son, that whoever believes in Him should not perish but have everlasting life." (John 3:16)

When we look at children, we must ask some questions. When can they decide to follow Christ? Is it possible for a young child to understand what it means to be lost and to receive Christ as their personal Savior and Lord? The answer is yes! Most people who put their faith in Christ worldwide do so between 4 and 14 years of age. This bracket is known as the "4/14 Window." [3]

One day I was visiting with a 5-year-old girl about her decision to accept Jesus Christ. We met in my office along with her mother. I asked her, "Why did you think that you needed to accept Jesus as your Savior?"

She said readily, "I am the worst sinner in the world, and I needed Jesus to come into my heart to save me from my sins. So, I accepted Jesus as my Savior and Lord."

Right then, I knew that the Holy Spirit was drawing this little girl to himself. Her understanding of sin and brokenness over sin let me know that the Holy Spirit revealed this to her. I then asked her, "Do you believe that Jesus died for your sins and rose on the third day (1 Corinthians 15:3-4)?" She said, "Yes, I do!"

Paul tells us, "That if you confess with your mouth the Lord Jesus and believe in your heart that God has raised Him from the dead, you will be saved. For with the heart one believes unto righteousness, and with the mouth, confession is made unto salvation" (Romans 10:9-10). From what she confessed, I understood that she had truly been born again (John 3:3). One evidence that we know when a child is drawn to Christ is the conviction of sin. Jesus tells us, "And when He has come, He (the Holy Spirit) will convict the world of sin, and of righteousness, and of judgment: of sin" (John 16:8-9a). Through the conviction of sin, a child can come to true repentance (Romans 2:4) and turn to God in their heart and life.

The wonderful message of the Gospel is simple, and children readily respond to it. It is basic but outstanding; it is also simple enough for a young child to lead their family and friends to Christ. Many of our younger children in our church were led to Christ by our preteens.

We had a policy at our church: when a child made a profession of faith, I was responsible for sitting down and listening to their story. I would ask where they were when they accepted the Lord. They would say at home, in the car, at camp, at Vacation Bible School, at church, etc. Then I would ask them who had led them to Christ, and they often said it was their mom, dad, or sibling.

When I talked with a child who had been counseled by one of our preteens, I rarely found that they did not understand their decision. We were very thorough in the training of our preteens. We taught them to ask all open-ended questions and how to discern if a person was not ready to accept Christ—not understanding sin or not being convicted of sin.

Kendall (11 years old) shared,

> When I became a Christian, I wasn't thinking only about going to Heaven. I saw others coming to Christ, and I saw their lives drastically change. One kid...he was always telling lies and blaming other people, and the next thing, he became a Christian. He was totally different, and I wanted to be that way because I knew that I sinned. I would go to church, and I thought that I was a good person, but I really needed to know Christ. And I knew that if I knew Him, I would change.

B. Sealed by the Holy Spirit

"In Him you also trusted, after you heard the word of truth, the gospel of your salvation; in whom also, having believed, you were sealed with the Holy Spirit of promise, who is the guarantee of our inheritance until the redemption of the purchased possession, to the praise of His glory." (Ephesians 1:13-14)

The moment the little girl I spoke of earlier believed in Jesus, the Holy Spirit sealed her for eternity.

1. She received THE HOLY SPIRIT, not a "baby" Holy Spirit.
2. She moved, in God's eyes, "from sinner to saint." [4]
3. She received God's seal of ownership.

Wiersbe writes, "What is the significance of this sealing of the Holy Spirit? For one thing, it speaks of a finished transaction. Even today, when important legal documents are processed, they are stamped with the official seal to signify the completion of the transaction. This sealing also implies ownership: God has put His seal on us because He has purchased us to be His own (1 Corinthians 6:19–20)." [5]

The infilling of the Holy Spirit is very real in the lives of children. Many times, I have personally witnessed a child change before my eyes. In the days and weeks after they accept Christ, I have seen the transformation. It becomes so evident of the new birth when they have a hunger for God's Word and the things of God. They desire to know Him, to grow in Him, and to live for Him.

C. The Holy Spirit Empowers Them

"But when the Helper comes, whom I shall send to you from the Father, the Spirit of truth who proceeds from the Father, He will testify of Me." (John 15:26)

The Holy Spirit works in so many different ways in children and students. I have watched preteens who were frightened and literally shaking minutes before they boldly spoke for God. There is a consistent, common thread. When a child is pushed out of what is comfortable for them, it triggers a crisis of belief.

That crisis causes them to humbly turn to the Father for help through prayer. Then, God shows up in powerful ways. The Spirit frequently speaks through them, which is evident in what they say. He will take them far beyond their abilities and gifts. "For the Holy Spirit will teach you in that very hour what you ought to say" (Luke 12:12).

I have heard countless testimonies of this movement of the Spirit during our mission trips. Here are a few testimonies from preteens who experienced the work of the Spirit in a variety of ways.

Once we started preaching…at that time, I was just shaking. I remember praying to myself and saying, 'God, I cannot do this by myself. This is all You.' I remember going brain dead at that point. I still to this day do not know exactly what I said. I just knew that He had given me a calling to go and teach. (Sarah, 11 years old)

About two minutes before I was going to share my testimony, God gives me a tap on my shoulder and says, 'No, that's not your testimony; its Mine.' So, I go up there, and I have no clue what I am going to say. But I just start talking. God basically said what I was going to say, but He helped me use props, which I had never done before. I thought that was kind of cool. It was really cool for God to speak directly to you and have Him speak to your heart. The kids took it really well because it was a message straight from God. (Katie, 11 years old)

I was speaking today, and I was saying, 'Ah, ah, what' and then later on, I surrendered. The Holy Spirit came over me, and I set down my book and said what was in the book from memory. Then they all latched on. (Josh, 12 years old)

I was supposed to tell the Bible story and was supposed to do things at Kids Blitz (evangelistic outreach). I had all of the pressure on me; I was freaking out. I was about to stop everything and say I don't want to do this anymore. I sat down, and I prayed, and God spoke to me and said, "Everything is going to be okay. You got this." (Pressley, 11 years old)

Peter reminds us of what is happening here. "But this is what was spoken by the prophet Joel: And it shall come to pass in the last days, says God, That I will pour out of My Spirit on all flesh; Your sons and your daughters shall prophesy" (Acts 2:17). In His perfect way, the Holy Spirit speaks through children.

As you have heard from the fascinating stories above, children often cannot describe what happened, but they are amazed by the Holy Spirit using them to testify about Christ. The Holy Spirit empowers children in different ways as they learn to listen to His leadership.

Following an evening service, one of our leaders, Art, came up to me and said, "You will not believe what just happened!" I asked, "What?" Art said, "I was sitting in the back of the service and feeling discouraged. I mentioned three things to the Lord that were heavy on my heart. Right after I prayed, Madeline tapped me on the shoulder. She said, 'Mr. Art, can I pray for you?' I said, 'Sure!' Then we moved to the middle of the room. She started praying, and she mentioned the three things I just inquired of the Lord about." Art and I were both shocked and amazed that day. This little girl listened to the Holy Spirit and obeyed His voice, resulting in a big blessing for Art.

D. The Holy Spirit Imparts Spiritual Gifts

"As I was doing my quiet time/devotional time this week, I got a chance to reflect. As I read God's Word, I wanted to share one of these passages with you that summarized what I have witnessed and experienced. 'As each one has received a gift, minister it to one another, as good stewards of the manifold grace of God' (1 Peter 4:10). It was amazing to see God's presence and the gifts just wowing from the group I was working with. Some were evangelists, some were teachers, some were comforters; it was just a joy. I wanted to share that with you and give God the glory."
—Parnel Ryan, preteen parent [6]

When does a person receive gift(s) from the Holy Spirit? When does a child receive spiritual gifts? Does it come when they turn 18 years of age? This question, at times, baffles the adult believer. "Too many Christians think that conversion is the only important experience and that nothing follows. But this is wrong." [7]

- The most significant way to discover the spiritual gifts of children is in ministry.

- Spiritual gifts in children and students manifest while they are ministering.

- Spiritual gifts will rarely manifest in a church where children and students just sit and listen and get ministered to by a leader.

To be true to the Word of God, the Spirit is the One who distributes spiritual gifts to the saints, and there is no age bracket that the Spirit follows. The criteria for distributing the Holy Spirit's spiritual gifts are personal belief in Jesus Christ as Savior and Lord. At that moment, the Spirit begins His sanctification work and gifts the saints for works of ministry.

"Now concerning spiritual gifts, brethren, I do not want you to be ignorant... Therefore I make known to you that no one speaking by the Spirit of God calls Jesus accursed, and no one can say that Jesus is Lord except by the Holy Spirit. There are diversities of gifts, but the same Spirit. There are differences of ministries, but the same Lord." (1 Corinthians 12:1, 3-5)

When the believing child says, "Jesus is Lord," it indicates the Holy Spirit is working in their life. "The confession 'Jesus is Lord' is the touchstone of the Spirit's genuine work in the community." [8] The journey begins for the believing child when the church helps them discover their gifts and intentionally helps them find ministry places in the body. Spiritual gifts give them identity and purpose in the Church.

Stadtmiller questions today's thinking within the Church. The idea that children are not old enough or mature enough to serve has had a crippling effect on their faith development. He says, "I'm not sure when or why it happened, but somewhere back in the Church's grand history, we decided that only certain elements of a full life in Christ are available to our kids. This is definitely true in regard to spiritual gifts in kids. At some point, someone put up a spiritual height chart, and generations of Christian kids have been missing out on the ride of their lives ever since." [9]

I have learned the following lessons about spiritual gifts in children:

- Samuel was approximately 12 years of age when he heard the voice of God speaking to him.
- David was a youth when he conquered Goliath.
- Josiah was 8 years old when he became King of Israel.
- Jesus began His ministry at age 12.

My deep longing is for ministry leaders to take this to heart. I will go even further here. The place where you will see the greatest manifestation of the spiritual gifts in children and students is on mission...outside your church. I pray that this indeed stretches people's thinking and moves them to action.

We have an army sitting and waiting to go to battle for the Lord. They only need to be equipped and released, and then they will change the world. Nelson asserts, "I believe that training preteens (children) as leaders is the most overlooked natural resource in the world." [10]

Children and Students Are the Church Today

Breanne came to me at the beginning of our mission trip. She was 16 at the time. I could tell she had something on her mind. She said, "Brother Clint, please step back and let us run the mission trip." At first, I thought to myself, "How dare she rebuke me, her pastor!" Then I began to realize that this was what I had trained them to do. Not to rebuke me, but to speak as a leader. Because I knew this, it was easy for me to release responsibility to her and the other teen leaders on the trip.

It was a joy for me to watch them take over. It was very natural. The Holy Spirit had gifted them with gifts of leadership, teaching, administration, helps, mercy, prophecy, teaching, and much more. They worked with about 120 preteens and leaders on this trip. As I became less, they became greater leaders and flourished in their gifts.

The adults watched in amazement at their leadership abilities. At the same time, they respected the teens as leaders because I gave them leadership roles and authority on the trip. When I gave them opportunities to minister, it strengthened their faith and gave them the confidence to do anything God would ask of them.

In my earlier days of ministry, I had no actual vision for children serving in the church. I regularly, year-after-year, went through the motions of ministry with very few objectives to accomplish. But when I witnessed their unique spiritual gifts and talents that God had given them, it changed my mind completely.

There are few discussions today concerning a child's role in the church; however, we must again look at the Word of God as our guide. If children are not mature enough to serve, why do they have spiritual gifts? If they have the gifts of administration, teaching, leadership, prophecy, and many more, then they, like all believers, have what is needed to serve in the body of Christ now.

The Church Is Called to Equip All the Saints

"And He gave some as apostles, and some as prophets, and some as evangelists, and some as pastors and teachers, for the equipping of the saints for the work of service, to the building up of the body of Christ." (Ephesians 4:11-13, NASB)

Paul shows us that church leaders are called to equip the saints for ministry (Ephesians 4:11-13). This passage of Scripture shows us that all believers (saints) are called to minister, not just a few leaders.[11] It clarifies that leaders are not to do all the work but to equip believers for the work, for ministry in the body. This calling includes children and students. As their leaders, we train children to minister in the body of Christ. [12] The saints, including children, are called to serve and minister alongside us. "But you are a chosen generation, a royal priesthood" (1 Peter 2:9).

In my early children's ministry years, I looked at children as the future Church—the FUTURE! But when I saw how God gifted them, it totally changed my view. Anders suggests, "Spiritual gifts are at the heart of Christ's strategy for building his church. [13] The gifts are ministers (or ministries) for the church." Building up the body of Christ "defines the nature of the work of ministry" and perfection comes through the process of building. [14]

Children and students can and should be considered a part of the Church today because they have God's seal of approval on them (Ephesians 1:13-14)—the Spirit of the living God. "To them, God willed to make known what are the riches of the glory of this mystery among the Gentiles: which is Christ in you, the hope of glory" (Colossians 1:27). Christ made His residence in their hearts, just like all believers. [15]

Remember, it is not a "baby" Jesus, but Jesus Christ Himself. "God has sent forth the Spirit of His Son into your hearts, crying out, 'Abba, Father!' Therefore you are no longer a slave but a son, and if a son, then an heir of God through Christ" (Galatians 4:6-7). They receive the whole package at the point of salvation; they are sealed, filled, gifted, and empowered for ministry and missions.

Pressley had been a Christian for about three years when her children's pastor allowed children to serve and minister at her church. During this time, they gave opportunities for children to teach during children's church. She would practice and prepare at home and teach on Sunday. It did not take long for her to discover that it was one of her spiritual gifts. As her children's ministers saw this, they began to give her even more teaching responsibilities. I observed her creativity one day as she was teaching 5-year-olds at church. Her originality amazed me, knowing that she was only 11 years old. She taught like an adult. She listened to God's leadership as she prepared her lesson. It was a blessing to observe Him speaking through her.

That summer during a preteen mission trip, she was asked to teach during an evangelistic event on the trip. Her leaders were working with her as she practiced her message. We could tell that she was very nervous and almost hyperventilating. We encouraged her to relax, be herself, pray, and let the Lord speak through her.

When she walked onto the platform that evening, there was a new bold confidence in her eyes. Pressley began her message, and it flowed beautifully. She preached the Gospel that evening, and many children trusted Christ as a result. I was utterly astonished by her, and I have not seen a more straightforward message given by an 11-year-old than Pressley's.

I no longer question whether a child has spiritual gifts—they do! We only have to help them discover their gifts and then equip and release them in ministry. I am suggesting that our children's and students' success in the body of Christ is of the utmost importance. Our mandate is the Great Commission, and they are to be included as co-equals in His commission.

Because they have God's seal of approval on them, they are children of the King of kings and Lord of lords. God can use any vessel that is available to Him. What would churches be like if children's and students' success were made top priority? Not to give them a beautiful facility, but to give them opportunities to serve using their gifts.

I cannot recommend more highly that this be every church's highest priority. What if the goal was to provide a platform for every child and student to minister? An opportunity for them to use their spiritual gifts for the glory of the Lord? The outcome would be quite amazing. Not only would they be invested in ministry at an early age, but they would stick around to continue doing so. Also, there would be no more leadership voids.

Children Are Disciple Makers

As I was looking down the children's hallway at my church, I saw one of our kids, Renee, walking towards me with a girl I did not recognize. She walked up to me and said, "Brother Clint, this is Jordan. She accepted Christ last night." I exclaimed, "Praise the Lord! Welcome to the family." As they walked away to their Bible study room, Renee's mother walked up to me. She said, "Clint, Renee has been leading a Bible study at our house for a year. Jordan's mother would not allow her to go to church, so Renee decided she would have a Bible study at our home for her. Last night, Renee led her to Christ." Renee was in 3rd grade at the time.

You might ask, "Is the Great Commission for all believers?" The answer is—Yes! The Great Commission is clear for all believers to make disciples of all nations (Matthew 28:19-20); this includes children!

1. Children are the most effective agents for reaching children in the 4 to 14 age bracket. [16]

2. Approximately 70 percent of those who accept Christ today say their peers influenced them. [17]

3. Most people who trust in Christ do so between the ages of 4 and 14 years. [18]

Knowing that they can effectively reach other children, they should be a part of the discipleship process. We can train them and send them out on a mission for Jesus Christ. Children are the mission field and the missionaries in that field. It is a joy to train and release them to go out on a mission for Christ.

- We are to equip children for ministry and release them to do ministry.
- There are no spiritual height charts.
- There are no age brackets.
- The Holy Spirit is the determining factor when He draws them to Himself.
- The only measuring rod is the Holy Spirit and what He can do in and through the life of a child or student.

I received a call from a nearby church one day. The children's minister was ecstatic. She told me about a 3rd-grade boy (9 years old) in her church named Timothy who felt called to be a missionary. He went to school and met a little boy who said he was an atheist. That afternoon, Timothy asked his mother if he could start a Bible study at his school to reach this little boy, and she said that was okay.

They went to the school and received permission. A few weeks later, Timothy started the Bible study. His older brother, who was a preteen, taught him how to conduct an evangelistic Bible study and lead someone to Christ. A few weeks later, Timothy started his Bible study at school.

During the study, he led the little atheist boy to Christ. Then a few weeks later, he led a little girl to Christ. He continued to teach them about Jesus and how to walk with Him. Both children started helping Timothy during his Bible study each week from then on.

While talking with children and leaders at New Beginnings Fellowship in Hollister, Missouri, I had a wonderful interview with a little girl named Brynleigh who was in 2nd grade at the time. She shared about how she and her friend led another little girl to Christ on the school bus. Here is her testimony:

> The other day on the bus, we were kind of just talking about Christian-type things and so we asked the girl next to us, Sydney, if she knew anything about Jesus and she said "no." And so me and Gracie just looked at each other and then we started telling her about Jesus. We just told her Bible stories, and some of them were just mixed all together at the same time. We told her a lot about Heaven, and then we told her all what would happen if she didn't know about Jesus. So, I said, "Do you want to go to Heaven?" And she said, "No." And I said, "Why?" And she said, "Well, I don't what to be with the devil." And I said, "Well, the devil was cast down to Hell because he didn't want to serve God." So then I said, "You'd only be with God." Then a couple minutes later after explaining all what would've happened, then we both said, "Do you want to go to Heaven?" And she said, "Yes." And then I prayed with her.

L.I.T. Taught Me to Be a Leader by *Holland Coleman (L.I.T. 2007-2008)*

When I was old enough to join L.I.T., I jumped at the opportunity to do for others what had been done for me. Looking back, the most amazing thing I learned was a degree of ownership that many adults think kids are not ready for. Although we were supervised, when it was time for a Kids Jam (children's worship) or Kids Blitz (community outreach), we were responsible for everything. That included transporting our equipment, managing the stage, setting up and tearing down the auditorium, leading worship, all the various performances, teaching, and the invitation. This taught me a great deal about leadership, taking the initiative, and working with others to accomplish something.

Most importantly, my time in L.I.T. taught me that the Gospel is not merely an idea or a story, but that Christ is living and active among His people today, and that if you want to experience intimacy with Christ, the best way to do that is by coming alongside Him and joining in His work. That same sense of fulfillment that I first tasted in L.I.T.—of working toward an eternal purpose—is why I'm currently in seminary today and eager to pursue full-time ministry.

CHAPTER 3

The Hole in the Gospel

"I know this may sound radical, but we are suggesting that all young people should be raised with the conviction that they are to be missionaries and that their primary goal is to use their gifts and resources to advance God's kingdom so that every tribe, nation, and people group have the opportunity to respond to their rightful king." —Ross and Hemphill [19]

I love all the stories of the Bible; they inspire me. I love watching children's eyes light up as they listen intently to every detail as told. Some teachers have taught the Bible with such a passion that kids were drawn into the story. They taught the stories so well you could almost imagine yourself there.

Some of the stories that inspired me the most were of God asking people to do the impossible and them responding to that call. Moses knelt before a burning bush and left with a calling to take part in the deliverance of Israel. Joshua completed what Moses started by leading the Israelites into the promised land. He must have been afraid. God told him, "Do not be afraid; do not be discouraged, for the Lord your God will be with you wherever you go" (Joshua 1:9b). Throughout the book of Acts, the Church boldly went out on a mission to proclaim the most incredible message of all time—the Gospel of Jesus Christ.

Joining Jesus' Story

"Go therefore and make disciples of all the nations, baptizing them in the name of the Father and of the Son and of the Holy Spirit, teaching them to observe all things that I have commanded you; and lo, I am with you always, even to the end of the age." (Matthew 28:19-20)

The Great Commission is the Great Commission. It is the beautiful message of the Good News of Christ. God sent His Son into the world to die for the sins of the world. Jesus is the cure for our sins. Each of us know someone who shared Christ with us. The Gospel did not stop with the disciples; it has continued to spread. From the Great Commission to now, the Gospel has been spreading worldwide with force.

Pressley's children's pastors had a leadership void, so they started training the preteens of her church to lead out. She eventually discovered that she had the gift of teaching. She began teaching when she was in 5th grade, and she attended a preteen mission trip that year. When she moved up into the student ministry, she felt out of place. There no longer were places in her church where she could serve.

She became burdened for the kids at her school, so she got permission from the school to lead a Bible study. At this point, Pressley has been teaching a Bible study at her school for more than three years. She is now in 9th grade, and she reaches many students with the Gospel. She averages about 40 students a week in her Bible study. She shared,

> When I moved up into student ministry, I wrestled with what I could do…I had this idea, and God was speaking to me. I had this amazing teacher. He sponsored me at the school. The Bible study started out sort of small. We had maybe 10 to 15 kids. They were listening and understanding. They started bringing their friends. They were being moved, and their hearts were being softened. It was just an amazing thing. It made me a lot more happy and excited because of the dark school we had—public school. It was cool to have this Bible study because no matter who you are or what you had done, you were invited to come and take what you need from it…The next year, we started back up again. That Bible study was ablaze. We had 40 kids coming and 4 got saved. We handed out over 30 Bibles to the kids who were coming.

Pressley's story is very common. When the Church embraces kids in view of God's purpose for them, they shine and develop personal confidence. Their confidence moves from the church building to the world at large. Their perspective of God's plan for their lives shifts and aligns with His purposes. From this newfound task, they discover God's will for their lives.

Shifting to True North

If you hold a compass in your hand, the main needle will point true north. People have navigated the seas and crossed countries with a compass. Our true north in the Church is Jesus Christ (Hebrews 12:2). He is our Focal Point for the body of Christ, our True North, our Commander and Chief. He has given an order, and He promises to empower those who obey that order (Acts 1:8).

I have witnessed God working in children, preteens, and students in unique ways, as I shared earlier. It has turned my whole perspective of the Church upside down. As I began to see young saints being used by God in powerful ways, I found a connection that was quite amazing. Unfortunately, somehow this is missing in the Church today. When my focus in children's ministry turned to Christ and His Commission, that is when I saw the Spirit of God show up in supernatural ways.

I found that God was frequently working directly opposite from what I had learned to do. I looked at children in age groups and believed they were able to do or comprehend only certain things about God, so we often put limitations on them. What I have discovered since, however, is that God can and will work in their lives when the adults get out of the way and allow Him to do so.

Sadly, we have become a hindrance to the children in our churches by putting limits on them based on age. In public education, this might be true; however, in the body of Christ, we are not constrained by age. Everyone receives the full package at new birth.

Age Is Not a Prerequisite to Serve God *by Sarah Gonzalez*
(L.I.T. 2013-2014)

I found myself wondering at times if younger children could be used by God as well. In the summer of 2013, I allowed some of the younger children in our churches to join us on our mission trip. They were trained the same as we trained our preteens. The Spirit of God used them to minister to children their age and older. Sarah was one of those who participated in that mission trip that summer. She shared,

The first time I went on a mission trip with Leaders In Training, I was seven years old. Even though I was the youngest child there, I quickly learned that age is not a prerequisite to serve God. That week, I saw God move firsthand in many powerful ways.

Over the years, I attended seven mission trips; however, I still remember the first time I gave the Gospel presentation. I was nervous, tired, and did not feel prepared to teach in front of a crowd. Before I started, my leader prayed for me, and at that moment the Holy Spirit took control. I don't remember what I said, but I remember feeling that God was using me to do His work and to glorify Him.

I am grateful to Leaders In Training because it taught me to understand that I have a responsibility to share the precious gift of salvation, and to do so, God is ready to use me as a vessel to glorify Him.

Throwing Children into the Deep End with God

While on a mission trip in Norman, Oklahoma, in 2010, I talked with leaders and parents beforehand about not rescuing preteens when they were fearful. We called it, "Throwing them into the deep end." It was so tempting to step in and protect them when times got tough.

Each day, teams met to plan out the next day of ministry at their ministry sites. A young preteen named Christina was with one of our ministry site teams. Her leader looked over at Christina and said, "Christina, you will teach the Bible study tomorrow." Christina instantly felt panicked and immediately ran to her mother and jumped in her lap in fear. Christina's mom, Nancy, pushed her away and said, "Christina, you are going to have to trust the Lord."

The next day, this team went out and set up their ministry site. They put the tarp down and got everything ready. The children gathered, and the preteens went through the worship songs and crafts with them. Then it was time for the Bible story. Christina stepped up and taught, and she took us all by surprise! This shy little preteen girl spoke in the power of the Holy Spirit. God used her gift of teaching to share His incredible story of redemption. The leaders all came back stunned by what they had witnessed. These leaders had become believers in walking alongside children and not allowing them to quit because of fear.

I want to help you understand that God has a plan, and by taking preteens in this direction, they will find their purpose in the Church. The truth is, we are on a mission to reach the world with the Good News of Christ. They can be a part of that story—the Great Commission—when we change the way we do ministry with them and start treating them as co-equals in the mission of God.

L.I.T. Has a Lasting Impact

When children and students find their purpose in the Church at a young age, we find that they most often continue to grow in the Lord and serve as they mature into adults. Channing Haye (former L.I.T.) shared how her time as an L.I.T. impacted her life through the years leading up to today:

> I did mission work, both local and international, in high school, college, and even now because I saw the importance of it early on in L.I.T. This has also now transferred to the workplace for me. Instead of approaching my job as a separate part of my life, I see it as a mission field. I ask God to provide and reveal opportunities for me to share about what God has taught me and His Good News.

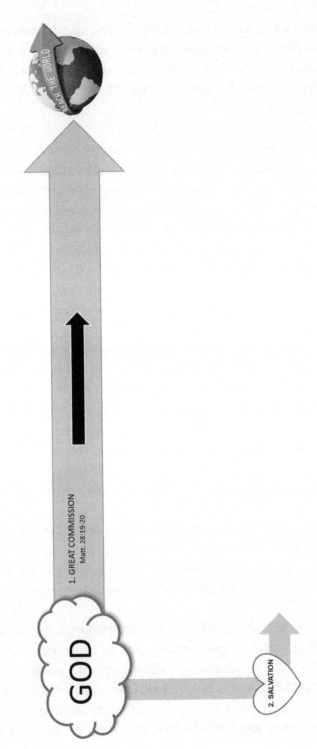

REACH THE WORLD

1. GREAT COMMISSION
Matt. 28:19-20

GOD

2. SALVATION

Sadly, many people will never experience Christ beyond making a profession of faith in Him. They will hear the message and respond; however, due to a lack of discipleship, they will remain babes in Christ for the remainder of their lives. Much of discipleship today is knowledge-based with no accountability or personal one-on-one mentorship. They never move from being mentees to mentors of others—disciple makers.

The Hole in the Gospel

"Bow your head, please. If you would like to accept Jesus as your Savior and Lord, pray this prayer with me, 'Lord Jesus, I know that I am a sinner. I know that You died for my sins and rose on the third day. Please forgive me for my sins. I ask You to come into my heart to be my Savior and Lord.'"

I led many children in this prayer in my first 13 years of ministry. Remember, I am a child evangelist at heart, and I want children to come to Christ and accept Him as their Savior. But my greatest sin was what happened afterward—NOTHING! I handed out Bibles and new Christian materials to them, but it just was not enough. I do not know how many Vacation Bible Schools, camps, special events, and retreats I have done that I walked away and did not follow up with the kids who made professions of faith. I AM GUILTY!

In the graphic on page 42, you see God and His eternal plan. The arrow coming down from God represents the Gospel. Many today have heard the Gospel and have accepted Christ as their Savior, having believed in Him. Notice that the arrow stops, though. That is what is happening to countless people. They attend a crusade, camp, revival, or special event, they pray to receive Christ, and then nothing. Salvation becomes the beginning and end of discipleship for them.

You see, guys, the Gospel is the most incredible message of all. When a person is born again, they become a child of God; they are a part of God's family. But it does not stop there. We must help show them how to walk with the Lord and grow in their faith every day of their lives. They need to know that God will not leave them alone, that they can call to Him in prayer at any moment, 24/7.

Our Creator saved us for a relationship with Him; we are His children, and nothing can remove us from His hands. These new believers need to learn these things—who they are in Christ and that He desires a daily relationship with them. They need to be trained and equipped for ministry in the church and the world today. They need to become disciple-makers themselves.

A New Identity in Christ

At the point of salvation, many things occur in the new believer's life. Yes, they will spend eternity with God in heaven after they die. But that is not the whole story. God gives them everything for life, victory, and to fulfill the great commission here on the earth. Here are just a few of the things that happen to a person at the point of new birth.

- They are born again. (John 3:3)

- They are called Saints. (Ephesians 4:11)

- They are sealed by the Holy Spirit. (Ephesians 1:13)

- They are gifted by the Holy Spirit. (1 Corinthians 12)

- They are children of God. (John 1:12)

- They have been given new life. (John 10:10)

- God is their heavenly Father. (Romans 8:14-15)

- They are no longer slaves of Satan but are God's children. (Colossians 1:13-14)

- They are empowered by the Holy Spirit. (Acts 1:8)

- They are seated in Heaven. (Ephesians 1:6)

- They are one in Christ. (Romans 12:5)

- They are a part of God's divine plan. (Matthew 28:19-20)

- They are saved, sanctified, and glorified. (Romans 10:9-10; 2 Thessalonians 2:13; Romans 8:30)

- They have God's divine nature. (Colossians 1:27)

- They have direct access to God. (Hebrews 4:16)

- They are ambassadors of Christ. (2 Corinthians 5:20)

- They are new creations. (2 Corinthians 5:17)

- They were crucified with Christ, and their sins are gone forever. (Galatians 2:20)

- Christ lives in them. (Colossians 2:6-10)

- They have been blessed with every spiritual blessing in Heaven. (Ephesians 1:3)

- Their bodies are temples. (1 Corinthians 6:19-20)

At new birth, they are given a new identity in Christ. The old has passed away, and they belong to Him now. Every believer in Christ has been brought into the family of God with a purpose—God's purpose. That purpose is not to be a spectator but an active part of the Great Commission. It is no wonder children and students are bored in church. They do not have any idea what they have or who they are in Christ.

Our calling is to disciple and equip them for ministry. We show children and students how to walk with Christ and join Him, along with all believers, to reach the world with the message of Christ. Heaven is a wonderful place, but we—and they—have work to do here on Earth. In His work, we find purpose and meaning for life—the life of a disciple of Christ.

One of my favorite professors in seminary, Dr. Roy Fish, said something that resonates in my heart even today: "If you lead a person to Christ and do not disciple them and teach them how to walk with Him, it is almost as bad as not leading them to the Lord at all. The enemy will eat them alive!"

The Lack of Discipleship Causes Confusion

One Sunday morning, I was in an adult Bible study class. Our teacher was ill, so the director had to improvise that morning. He shared, "Our teacher is out, so what I would like for us to do this morning is to share our testimonies." One-by-one, men and women stood and shared how they came to know the Lord.

The first person shared, "I was at a church about 7 years ago. When I heard the invitation, I walked forward and talked with someone. I accepted Christ that day. After that, I felt baffled and frustrated; I did not know what was next. I became angry with God and stopped going to church from that point on. When I came to this church, I did it all again. But this church has been very loving and accepting, and I have been here ever since."

The next three testimonies were very similar. Each person had prayed a prayer to receive Christ, but they never had anyone come alongside them and show them how to walk with Christ daily. I can raise my hand and say that it happened to me as well.

We Do Not Stop at Salvation

I am all for evangelizing the lost, but that is the starting point of discipleship, not where we stop in our walk with Christ. I want new believers to join Christ on His great adventure for their lives. I want them to discover His plan and purpose for why they were created and allow them to fulfill God's plan in the church and in the world. I want to make disciples who make disciples. Only then have we fulfilled God's calling for the Church (Matthew 28:19-20).

God has a purpose for each person's life. He chose us. The very fact that we came to know Christ is the work of the Holy Spirit. "He came to convict the world of sin and unrighteousness" (John 16:8). But salvation is not the end of the story. There is a cost to follow Jesus—that cost is your life. Jesus calls everyone who desires to put their faith in Him to deny themselves and follow Him (Luke 9:23).

I struggled with this when I was 27 years old. I was a convert, but it was almost 18 years later after I had accepted Him that the Lord made it clear He wanted all of my life. After struggling, I knelt beside my bed in October 1984 and said, "I surrender my life to You. I will do whatever You ask me to do." That act of surrender in my personal life completely transformed my life and started me down the path where I am today.

I surrendered my life to the Lord that day. I thought I was giving up "everything," but He gave "everything" back to me and so much more. That is what I want for the kids in my church—in your church. I want them to have an encounter with the living Christ. I want them to be saved, but I want them to give their lives to Christ and become part of Christ's story for their lives. I want them to have the joy I have found in following Him. Bosher put it this way, "He gave His all, and He expects for you to give your all."

I Had a Fire in My Heart *by Madison Miller (L.I.T. 2008-2010)*

When I was in 5th grade, I started Leaders In Training. During that time, I learned how to make my faith my own and share it with others. On my first L.I.T. mission trip, God used me to lead a girl my age to Christ. From that moment on, I had a fire in my heart for sharing my faith and ministering to the kids around me.

From 5th grade to now, I have had the opportunity to invest in and disciple children. I started off by teaching a Sunday school class when I was in 6th grade. I was a Children's Intern in college. Now, I work as part of a kids' ministry.

Spiritual Maturity at a Young Age *by Breanne Morgan Galey (L.I.T. 2009-2010)*

Throughout my two years in L.I.T. (and the many years of returning to serve as a leader that followed), I learned in depth what utilizing my talents in ministry looked like, how to share the Gospel personally and effectively, how to pray, how to study Scripture, and how to overall orient my life towards the scriptural teachings, disciplines, and callings God has for Christians. I was learning how to fall into the rhythm of a relationship with God (a big deal for a 12-year-old!).

I feel that I developed a spiritual maturity at a young age that I never would have otherwise. It is because of L.I.T. that I feel I've been able to start the Gospel conversation in so many relationships I've had throughout high school, college, and now in my adult career with ease and confidence. It has always stuck with me that it's not my job to convict or bring salvation upon any person, but that God equips me with the Good News and brings the joy and confidence I need to share, without any personal pressure for an outcome. I truly believe that because I was able to practice sharing the Gospel so many times at such a young age (both in the safe setting of a Bible study group and with other kids I met at outreach events) that I've been able to share with such ease ever since.

CHAPTER 4

Spiritual Revelation:

Raising Up a
Kingdom-Focused Generation

Spiritual revelation is a striking or conscious disclosure of something not realized about God and His will for the believer in Christ.

While observing spiritual encounters with God in children, a common theme occurs when focusing on discipling and equipping them for ministry. We move them out of what is comfortable into a new reality with God. We want them to have that crisis of faith that causes them to trust the Heavenly Father. That unique experience causes a spiritual revelation, a divine encounter, and it sets their spiritual foundation deep—God reveals Himself to and through them.

Children personally have revelations of God in their lives when we break out of what is standard practice in the church today. When we move them to a new typical—to the Great Commission—they will experience God in ways that they never will see by staying inside the church building. The Holy Spirit empowers them in the midst of ministry and missions.

Observation of Spiritual Revelation in Preteens

The chart on the next page shows our observation when a child moves from accepting Christ to Lordship. At the point of surrender, there appears to be a rapid transformation in their life. Many will have a powerful encounter with God at the point of making the holy sacrifice of laying down their lives to the Master (Romans 12:1).

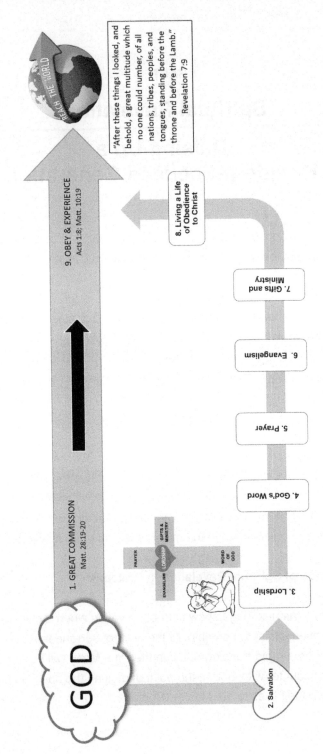

"After these things I looked, and behold, a great multitude which no one could number, of all nations, tribes, peoples, and tongues, standing before the throne and before the Lamb."
Revelation 7:9

9. OBEY & EXPERIENCE
Acts 1:8; Matt. 10:19

8. Living a Life of Obedience to Christ

7. Gifts and Ministry

6. Evangelism

5. Prayer

4. God's Word

3. Lordship

PRAYER   GIFTS & MINISTRY
LORDSHIP
EVANGELISM   WORD OF GOD

1. GREAT COMMISSION
Matt. 28:19-20

GOD

2. Salvation

One of the keys to spiritual revelation, or the starting point, is surrendering one's life to Christ. It moves the child, or person, into an immediate encounter with the living Christ. One of the missing elements of discipleship is surrender. Let us look at discipleship in view of the bigger picture of the Great Commission. There is a purpose for why we are here and a clear call and direction we are to take as the body of Christ. Every believer is called to obey Christ's commands (Matthew 28:19-20). Here is what we have observed:

1. **The Great Commission:** Jesus' command before His ascension is to GO and make disciples of all nations. Our purpose is to fulfill His calling in obedience to Him. We are heading to the end of the story, when every tribe, nation, and tongue stands before the throne of God and the Lamb (Revelation 7:9). If your ministry is not experiencing God's power and presence, you may be doing other things rather than fulfilling the Great Commission. We cannot do church as usual when more than three billion people have never heard the Gospel even one time. God's master plan includes the whole body of Christ. Jesus left us with a commission: "Go and make disciples." Unfortunately, the word "GO" is hard for many to embrace. No wonder so many of our churches are powerless, plateaued, and dying.

2. **Salvation:** Christ died for the sins of the world, and by personal belief in His death, burial, and resurrection, we have eternal life (John 3:16, 2 Corinthians 15:3-4). As we shared, children are the most significant harvest field worldwide. From salvation, we move them to total surrender to God. I have personally counseled many children who were deeply broken over their sin and turned to Christ to save them from their sin.

3. **Surrender:** Children should be called to make a holy sacrifice to God—surrender (Romans 12:1). Surrender is not a choice to do or not do—it is expected. If you want to follow Christ, you must lay down your life, deny yourself, take up your cross, and follow Him (Luke 9:23). Remember, when you give Christ your all, He gives

so much more in return. Do you not want the kids in your church to experience the same thing? They can if you lead them down this path. Many things happen at the point of surrender that are quite amazing. In some ways, it is a similar experience for each child, but it can also be very different from one child to another. We have observed approximately 3,000 preteens on mission for Christ in the past 20 years. From what we have seen, this is a holy moment that results in brokenness.

4. **Brokenness:** There appears to be a clear experience of the presence of God for preteens that immediately brings conviction of sin and brokenness. They are not sure what is happening to them, but they feel God's presence. When Isaiah was taken up into the presence of God and he heard the angels crying out in worship, "Holy, Holy, Holy," there was an immediate conviction of sin. He said, "Woe is me, for I am undone! Because I am a man of unclean lips" (Isaiah 6:5a). Marc (adult leader) stated, "We have seen our kids broken over their sins. They don't understand what is happening." Bobby (5th grade) shared, "God took away all of my sins, and I am ready to tell people about Him."

5. **Intercession:** When children are broken, there appears to be a new boldness in approaching God and the throne of grace (Hebrews 4:16). There is a new confidence, knowing that their hearts are right before Him. They naturally come together and pray for each other with a new authority and confidence. They pray to overcome their fears. They often circle up, lay hands on someone who may be hurting, and pray over them.

   Intercession for Family Members—We have observed on many occasions that brokenness leads to intercession for lost family members. Believing children become more aware of their own sins as well as the sins of others. Isaiah declared, "I live amongst a people with unclean lips" (Isaiah 6:5b).

I observed a group of girls in a circle crying and weeping. I asked them, "Is everything okay?" Sarah (5th grade) answered, "I was so worried about my uncle's salvation that I was praying for him, and I could not stop crying." Sandi (adult leader) shared, "We have a prayer room for our preteens. One day, one of the girls found out that her uncle was lost. She and the other kids in the room cried out for her uncle's salvation."

Intercession for the Lost—Preteens quickly move from praying for family members to praying for the lost. There appears to be a transition after they experience brokenness to an urgency for them to tell others about God's grace and forgiveness. They meet lost people, and many times, they weep and cry for their salvation. One of the adult leaders shared, "They quickly take on the burdens of the children they met. They cried for hours over the kids at the sites." Brandi (adult leader) shared, "I have been on youth mission trips where we made repairs and fixed things up, but never anything like this."

Spiritual Warfare—We have observed preteens gain confidence from the Lord and learn to listen to the Holy Spirit. We encouraged leaders to step back and allow the children to listen to the Holy Spirit and do what He leads them to do.

On a mission trip, one of our teams had no children from the apartments coming to their Bible study. They would faithfully go out and go through their planned activities (songs, games, crafts, etc.), hoping for children to come each day. I told them that we don't always have lost people attending church, but we worship together and hear God's Word taught. So, that is what they did; they worshipped and went through their whole Bible study together each day.

On the third day, one of the preteens suggested that they march seven times around the swimming pool at the apartments and sing the song *Undignified* (by David Crowder Band). The leader said, "Let's do it!" As they marched around the pool, the maintenance man thought they were crazy. They finished their march and headed to the clubhouse to start their Bible study.

They went in and set up the room and got everything ready, but no kids showed up. About 15 minutes later, three children walked up to the door. The preteens were so excited that they scared the younger of the three. By the end of the Bible study time, two children received Christ as their Savior and Lord. It sounded like a crazy idea, but the kids listened to the Holy Spirit, and the Lord sent children to their Bible study.

6. **Boldness to Share:** We have observed on multiple occasions children emboldened with the Gospel after they surrender to Christ. Jerry (adult leader) shared in tears, "God convicted my heart today. He revealed to me that I am a coward. These kids were fearless, and they went door to door sharing Christ while I stood in the distance afraid." Todd (adult leader) shared in tears, "After what I have observed, I have had to ask the Lord to forgive me for not having a burden for the lost. The kids have taught me a lot. I am going home with a new commitment to share the Gospel with people I encounter."

7. **God Speaks to Them and Through Them:** Jesus tells us, "Do not worry beforehand, or premeditate what you will speak. But whatever is given you in that hour, speak that; for it is not you who speak, but the Holy Spirit" (Mark 13:11). We have observed that children are fearful about sharing their testimony or a Bible study on many occasions. In their fear, they turn to the Heavenly Father for help.

Jordan (12 years old) shared, "I was supposed to teach today. I was really afraid. I prayed, 'Oh God, oh God, please help me, please help me.' Then I said something that I don't even know what I said." Katie (11 years old) explained, "I was teaching today. I was scared and got over in the corner to pray. When I got up to speak, God spoke through me in a powerful way. I don't even know what I said." What I have found is that many times God speaks through them, and they do not know what they shared. We have recorded many testimonies that are consistent in this way. What the kids experience is real even though they do not fully understand what God did through them.

One evening, a deacon from one of the churches that attended our mission trip in Fort Worth spoke of what he witnessed: "Shelly taught today, and she did an amazing job. A mother joined us today with her daughter and granddaughter. Shelley taught and then gave an invitation and asked those who wanted to trust Christ to raise their hand. The mother, daughter, and granddaughter all raised their hand. Shelley sat down on the curb with them and led three generations to Christ today."

8. **Manifestation of Spiritual Gifts (1 Corinthians 12; Ephesians 4:11-13):** We have observed the manifestation of spiritual gifts while doing ministry and missions. The children's gifts will naturally appear before your eyes when on a mission or serving in ministry. There are many gifted leaders among our kids, and they will naturally rise to the occasion when the opportunity presents itself.

We train every preteen attending the mission trips to teach the Bible study. Leaders quickly recognize the gifts of teaching that some of them have. Many times, leaders are astounded when they hear kids teach. Kevin, one of the adult leaders on a trip, explained, "Mark got up to teach. He kind of stumbled around at first and then got really clear. When he finished, he put his Bible under his arm and gave an invitation."

Nine-year-old Carilyn had the gift of administration. She started out organizing our resource room. Then, I put her in charge of our bus ministry, where she called about 30 children every week. I began to take her on our mission trips with us. She took over the administrative tasks, such as applications, food orders, and reservation confirmations. When she first started with the bus ministry, she was 12 years old, and I could give her my credit card to order food or make a reservation without my help. She was an exceptional, gifted leader. She was very familiar with the ins and outs of the mission trips and became a key leader at a very young age.

9. **They Grasp God's Will:** It is apparent that children embrace the Word of God even more when they experience the Word of God. You can teach it, but we have observed them grasping it even more when they live it out. They can personally participate in prayer, serving others, using spiritual gifts, and evangelism. God says it, and they experience His promises.

Many begin to understand Scripture for the first time, whereas others have a more profound revelation of God's wisdom and purpose for the body of Christ and His plan for their lives. I have heard numerous kids say they understood the meaning of the Bible for the first time in their lives.

For example, God invites us to pray and call to Him. "Call to me and I will answer you, and will tell you great and hidden things that you have not known" (Jeremiah 33:3). Prayer is not something we teach about; we just do it. We pray—talk with God. After we arrived at our destination on one of our mission trips, we found out that a young man who was with us did not know Christ. Besides that, he did not even want to know the Lord.

After he left the worship center one evening, I gathered a group of our preteens together to pray for him. They started praying for Robert, and they were deeply burdened in prayer for his salvation. As they prayed, I had peace in my heart that Robert would trust Christ that week. I closed out the prayer time and sent the preteens to their rooms.

That very evening, Robert knelt and prayed to receive Christ. The next day, his countenance had completely changed from anger to joy. You could see that he was different. The kids on the trip were somewhat frightened as they had never seen a person transform overnight. Robert went out the next day and shared his testimony with joy.

One year, we began praying for the nations in the 10/40 Window. "Approximately 5.21 billion individuals residing in 8,874 distinct people groups are in the revised 10/40 Window. 6,170 (69.5%) of these people groups are considered unreached and have a population of 3.16 billion. This means approximately 61% of the individuals in the 10/40 Window live in an unreached people group. The 10/40 Window is home to some of the largest unreached people groups in the world such as the Shaikh, Yadava, Turks, Moroccan Arabs, Pashtun, Jat and Burmese." [20] On our recent mission trips, we have started praying for the 10/40 Window. When preteens see the number of lost people in this region, they are brokenhearted.

10. **Obey and Experience:** When a child surrenders their life to Christ, they move into a new reality with a more profound understanding of God's purpose for them and the Church. They become "doers of the word" (James 1:22). Amid obedience to Christ, there is great joy as they experience His presence in their lives. They embrace God's story—their story. They find their purpose and His purpose for their lives. They join the mission, the Great Commission, with a dream to see the whole world reached with the Gospel of Christ. Their goal becomes that every nation, tribe, and tongue will one day stand before God and the Lamb to worship (Revelation 7:9).

We Are Called to Make Disciples—That Is Our Calling

We can talk about the many beautiful stories of the Bible; however, God wants to create an extraordinary story with our children. They discover who God is through spiritual revelation. The Church's calling is to make disciples and missionaries for the Gospel. The more we train and release children for ministry, the more they have divine encounters with their Maker.

We will focus on significant events that bring spiritual revelation into a child's life. The greater manifestation of the Spirit of God occurs, in my observation, on mission sharing the Gospel—being in and doing the will of God. We have seen significant movements of the Spirit in their lives. When children are away from what is comfortable, they become more focused on God for help and deliverance.

Children Can Swim

"He (God) calls you to an assignment you cannot do without Him. The assignment will have God-sized dimensions. When God asks you to do something that you cannot do, it causes a crisis of belief. Can He and will He do what He has said He wants to do through you?" —Henry Blackaby [21]

Challenging children and pushing them out of what is secure for them causes a "crisis of belief." When Moses stood before God, there was a spiritual revelation. God chose him to be His agent to deliver Israel from Egypt. It became a debate between God and Moses. But God had His way, and Moses became the leader God wanted him to be. Moses had a crisis of belief until he stepped into God's will for his life. [22] Land and Trip share, "God is simply taking you where you do not want to go to produce in you what you could not achieve on your own." [23]

My friend Darla shared with me one day how she learned to swim. I thought she probably went to a public pool somewhere and took lessons. She said that her uncle taught both her and her brother: "We were at my uncle's house one day, and he indicated that he was going to teach us how to swim. He grabbed both of us by the collar and threw us into the deep end of the swimming pool, and hollered, 'SWIM!'" She said, "We swam with him standing there and coaching as we almost drowned."

When you push children into things that make them uncomfortable in ministry and on mission for God, many dynamics occur:

- You are forcing them past what is comfortable so that they turn to their Heavenly Father for help.
- They cry out to God, and He answers their prayers.
- The God of the impossible shows up and does the unthinkable through them.
- When you give a child a challenging task, many times their gifts manifest as they minister.
- Spiritual gifts come alive during ministry and missions.

Children need loving and caring adults who are willing to take them deeper and deeper with Christ. They do not rescue the kids but simply walk alongside them. Stadtmiller shares, "When they experience God in their giftings, they will be established in their faith, and they will begin to create a history of experiences in which God has backed up their faith with His manifested presence." [24]

We Hate That Look You Have

I love working with students. I took many of them along on our preteen mission trips, and they have taught me plenty. Their faith is strong, and they are a joy to work with. They amaze me with their wisdom and insight. They bring loads of knowledge to the table if you only allow them to take the lead or listen to their counsel.

On mission trips, I ask students to do challenging assignments, like sharing their testimony, teaching devotionals, or leading out with adults. They tell me, "We hate that look you have when you are going to ask us to do something hard." I learned that constantly pushing them to do what seems impossible for them causes them to turn to God for strength, and they come through every time.

One day, Breanne (a student leader) came to me and said, "I know what you are doing. You are giving me such a huge task that seems impossible to me. Then after I complete it, I find myself looking for the next big thing that God will do in my life." She got it! I made a point to train my leadership to push children out of what was easy to them, and the results were always the same. God encounters. Spiritual revelation.

Properly Equipped Leadership

The key to a child's or student's success is having adequately-trained adult leaders. These leaders know that it is essential NOT to rescue children and students from trials. However, they do stand with the kids as they walk through these experiences with the purpose of allowing them to encounter God in newfound ways through ministry and missions. One of three things happens as a result:

- Children experience the Holy Spirit's presence firsthand.
- Children witness and experience the Word of God and know that it can be trusted.
- Children study the Word of God and believe it to be true.

Leader Becomes Encourager/Mentor

A group leader, Katherine, applied what she learned in our training. She did not allow her team to escape or back out of their responsibilities of teaching or testifying on the mission trip. She shared,

I have seen my team as we prepared on certain days become fearful, whether it was about sharing their testimony or teaching a certain lesson. Sometimes they came to the point of tears. We have a majority of girls on our team, with one male. I have seen them riding on the bus, saying, 'I can't do this today. Don't make me do this today.' Through prayer and encouragement, God has shown up in huge ways and used them. Honestly, on the day that they were most afraid is when I have seen God work the most through them. I had some girls that were afraid, but they relied on God for strength and courage, and they pushed through. When everything seemed impossible, you think that you are not the right person. But by trusting in God, He will pull you through. After the girls ministered, we had five kids who wanted to know more about trusting Christ as their Savior. [25]

What if Katherine had taken the approach of the overprotective leader? What if when the girls got scared and begged her not to make them teach, Katherine took over to protect them? What if she had taught the lesson and done everything for them? What would these girls and one boy in her group have missed? A divine encounter—spiritual revelation.

Every time we become overprotective with children and students, we rob them of an opportunity to experience God's presence and power in ministry. Katherine stuck to the idea of pushing them into the depths with God. As they were fearful and overwhelmed, they prayed, trusted God, and He used them in powerful ways.

Here are some steps to take to help children walk through their crisis of belief and spiritual challenges in ministry:

1. Assign them challenging tasks
   (i.e., teaching, leading, prayer, testimonies, etc.).
2. When they become fearful, remind them to turn to the Lord for strength.
3. Pray with them for God's presence and power.
4. Walk alongside them and encourage them as they go through it.

Jesus Came Alive for Me *by Sarah Owens Langer (L.I.T. 2007-2008)*

Jesus came alive for me during my journey through L.I.T as a young girl. He was no longer a nice idea or a story, but a Father, a friend, and the safest place I have ever come to know. I am endlessly thankful for the opportunities I was given not only to experience God at work firsthand, but to engage in that work with Him at such a young age.

I was offered lifelong guidance in pursuing wisdom and discernment through discipleship, empowered to stand up with boldness and confidence in the face of adversity, and inspired to live a life of endless adventure in pursuing that which is true, good, beautiful, and worthy of praise in this life! I could go on and on about how formative this program was and continues to be in my life as an adult- in short, it was foundational. Programs like this not only empower the next generation of the Church, but it equips them with knowledge of what it means to faithfully follow Jesus to the end of their days.

CHAPTER 5

Taking Children into the Spiritual Depths Through Spiritual Disciplines

"The classical disciplines of the spiritual life call us to move beyond surface living into the depths. They invite us to explore the inner caverns of the spiritual realm. They urge us to be an answer to a hollow world."
—Richard Foster [26]

To understand where I am coming from and my passion, I want to share my story. When I was nine years old, my pastor led me to Christ. Shortly afterward, I was baptized. I grew up listening to Bible stories and sermons in church; however, there was very little change in my life. You might say I had a weak faith or did not know that there was anything beyond salvation.

Even as an adult, I tried to spend time in Scripture every day, but my life was powerless. The Lord never gave up on me. I was going through some tough times in my life, and I had to make a choice whether to follow Christ or not. Lordship was a foreign concept to me. However, in October of 1984, I knelt by my bed and said, "Lord, I surrender to You. I will do whatever You want." When I made Christ Lord of my life, everything changed. I was different overnight.

It All Suddenly Made Sense to Me

Before, when I would read Scripture, it seemed dull, meaningless, and hard to grasp. Then, it was as if a lightbulb flipped on in my mind; it all suddenly made sense to me. I found myself reading my Bible all through the night. I couldn't wait to go to church. Worship was real. I sat in the service mesmerized by God's love and grace. I had a new life, the abundant life, and I was not the same.

Over time, I felt the Lord calling me to ministry. I thought about it day and night. When I started seminary, I began to understand more about the abundant life that Jesus promised (John 10:10). I wanted others to have what I had. I wanted to help them down a path of surrendering their lives to Christ in a living relationship with the Master.

As I studied, I began to read books on discipleship. I read two books that gave me a deeper understanding of discipleship: *MasterLife* by Avery Willis and *Disciples Are Made Not Born* by Walter A. Henrichsen. They both talk about a relationship with Christ with six key components: lordship, God's Word, prayer, evangelism, fellowship, and obedience.

Before I read these books, I was personally living these out in my own life, and I was growing in my faith. They put everything into perspective for me. They helped me understand that these disciplines are key to spiritual growth and a sustaining faith for life. This was the missing piece that I had not been teaching kids for the previous 13 years of ministry.

A Burden for Discipleship

As time moved forward, I began to develop more of a strategy. I became deeply burdened for the child that would trust in Christ but never grace the step of a local church. This was when I began to write new Christian materials, which were basic resources that would help them in their new walk with Christ. The booklet included the six key disciplines mentioned above.

As I continued this new ministry path, one component seemed to be missing from the formula for growth—gifts and ministry. It was evident to me that these brought about fellowship as children ministered together. The more they served, the more their spiritual gifts manifested in their lives. This gave them identity and purpose. It allowed them to be a part of the Church.

Leaders In Training Begins

The summer of 2002 began a new venture in ministry for me. L.I.T. (Leaders In Training) was the name of our new preteen ministry model. Our desire was to disciple and equip preteens in partnership with their parents. That summer, if a preteen wanted to be involved in L.I.T., they would be required to have a daily quiet time with the Lord. We helped families prioritize their child's spiritual walk with Christ to be number one in their homes.

At church, we met with them in small discipleship groups to learn more about what they had studied at home. The disciplines they were learning at home were also reinforced with their leaders at the church. We also trained them to minister through puppets, worship, and serving others.

Now to the good part! When the preteens began spending time at the feet of the Master daily, they began to transform and change within the first four to six weeks. I had written a six-week devotional that incorporated the six disciplines mentioned earlier: lordship, God's Word, prayer, evangelism, fellowship, and obedience. Those six weeks went by quickly, so I started writing new devotionals every week. Within two years, I had written two years of materials.

L.I.T. Devotionals Transformed Their Lives

Flori (parent) shared how L.I.T. devotionals changed her daughters' lives.

It's not just a daily devotion talking about the Bible, but the Bible verses devote you daily to talking with God! I was searching for a devotion for my two girls that would take them into a living relationship with God, and when I found L.I.T., I could not wait to see the fruit of it. L.I.T. has made it all possible: the understanding of the Word, the fun of searching out the answers found in the daily scriptures, the knowing of their identity in Christ, the prayers they learned to say, and the putting into action of the Word of God!

Three years later, I am blessed and honored to say that my girls fully believe in God! They are disciples of Jesus, and they do weekly with other kids the same study that transformed their lives. It is working! They increased in their confidence to be leaders and their boldness to step out and minister to others. It has made them more aware of their purpose on this earth towards others. Other kids connected very well with the simplicity of their sharing of the Word, which caused other kids to do what they do.

The blessing of that first summer for me was to see many of our preteens' lives changed. The combination of developing their personal walk with Christ and participating in ministry made a huge difference in who they were as Christians. Their faith, like mine, came alive after aligning with the calling from the Lord to lay down their lives in surrender to His will (Luke 9:23).

Channing Haye (former L.I.T.) reflected on the discipline of having a daily quiet time as an L.I.T.:

Honestly, I really appreciated the structures and routines we were taught to be in God's Word and praying daily...Being able to share what we learned throughout the week was an opportunity for accountability as well as growing with one another. As an adult now, I do appreciate having a way to evaluate and discern the Scriptures.

I found the missing piece to discipling children, and I have been on this path now for more than 20 years. What joy it is to reach them with the Gospel and to see them begin their walk with Christ. Many children that were sitting in limbo in churches are now experiencing new life as they learn to walk with Christ daily.

Jamie (5th grade) shared her story of how she found Christ during outreach and how the following summer she went on her first mission trip to share Christ:

I was actually really excited that I got to come, and I have been really happy throughout the last year and this summer. I am thinking that's pretty cool that I started out being one of the kids who came to know Christ and then came to our church. Then I got to share with other people the next summer on a mission trip.

Lordship Is Not a Choice—It Is Expected

"Then He said to them all, 'If anyone desires to come after Me, let him deny himself, and take up his cross daily, and follow Me. For whoever desires to save his life will lose it, but whoever loses his life for My sake will save it. For what profit is it to a man if he gains the whole world, and is himself destroyed or lost?'" (Luke 9:23-25)

The Gospel cost Jesus everything. He suffered a horrendous death on the cross for the sins of the world. When He said, "It is finished!" He made a way to restore our relationship with God. Three days later, the stone rolled away, and Jesus walked out of the tomb victorious over sin, death, and hades. Jesus was willing to pay it all to restore what was lost in the Garden of Eden at the beginning of time.

Paul tells us, "For I delivered to you first of all that which I also received: that Christ died for our sins according to the Scriptures, and that He was buried, and that He rose again the third day according to the Scriptures" (1 Corinthians 15:3-4). It was God's plan from the beginning.

Jesus tells us that there is a cost to be His disciples. "Whoever of you does not forsake all that he has cannot be My disciple" (Luke 14:33). The cost is our life. But here is the catch in all of this: When we give up everything and follow Him, He gives us everything back and more. The very things we hang on to in this world do not bring life. Surrender equals life—the abundant life.

The most important first step in spiritual disciplines is Lordship. To take the step of surrender is to take the step into the living water (Ezekiel 47:1-5). This is where we want the children in our church to be. I want every child to understand God's plan for them, and through surrender, their lives will move in power.

- Surrender opens their hearts to understand the Word of God.

- Surrender is holy and pleasing to God.

- Surrender quickly brings them to the throne of grace in prayer.

- Surrender empowers their gifts.

- In surrender, the Spirit of God flows freely through their gifts as they minister in the church and to the lost world.

In Chapter 4, I shared that there is a spiritual revelation that occurs in children's lives through surrender. It quickly moves them to a new spiritual awareness of God and His purpose and plan for their lives. Here is the process I have observed children go through when they surrender to the Lordship of Jesus Christ:

1. Brokenness over sin

2. Intercession for the lost

3. God speaking to them and through them

4. Boldness to share the Gospel

5. Spiritual gifts manifested in ministry

6. Grasping God's will and the Great Commission

Martha (L.I.T. 2006-2007) shared,

I remember just crying as I made that choice to surrender. The release that it was and the freedom that it gives. You don't have to be nitpicking about your life. It's all in God's hands. When you surrender everything—your fears, your hopes, and your dreams—then you are open to what God wants you to do. In that path is the greatest joy. You know, until we surrender, there is no way we can live for Christ if He is not Lord of our life. That is what L.I.T. really stresses. Let Jesus be Lord of your life. Not just your Savior but your Lord. Surrender to Him and let Him guide your life, and experience being a child of God.

Out of Egypt into the Promised Land—Lordship

Let me illustrate what I see happening in many churches today. Remember the children of Israel and their bondage in Egypt for about 430 years (Exodus 12:40-41)? At God's chosen time, He called Moses to go to Pharoah and demand their release. Pharoah was not going to give in, so God sent 10 plagues upon Egypt. The final straw was the death of the firstborn of the Egyptians.

When Pharoah sent the Israelite people out, God gave them a favor—He allowed them to plunder Egypt (Exodus 12:36). Israel was delivered from the hands of Pharoah. They were in bondage to him, but then they were set free. They headed towards the shore of the Red Sea, and they felt the freedom as they journeyed out of sight of Egypt. They were free.

But Pharoah conjured the plan to go after them and bring them back to Egypt. He rallied his army and headed out to capture the Israelites. Can you imagine him calling out to his leadership: "Get my chariot and round up the army!"? He gathered them together, and they charged out after Israel. As they approached the people of Israel, God thwarted their effort by setting up a pillar of clouds by day and of fire by night. Pharoah and his army were stopped dead in their tracks.

During the evening, God parted the waters of the Red Sea. The next day, the people of Israel crossed through the sea on dry land. After the entire nation of Israel had crossed, God raised up the pillar of cloud so that the Egyptians would pursue them, crossing through the Red Sea after the Israelites. At that point, God released the waters, and Pharaoh's army was consumed. The people of Israel witnessed a great deliverance from a loving and powerful God.

Now let us look at it from this perspective. We were in darkness, and God brought us into the kingdom of the Son of God (Ephesians 2:1-2; Colossians 1:16). We were in bondage to Satan, and now we are free.

When the Israelites crossed over the Red Sea, they were saved from the hands of Pharoah forever—this is salvation. They were no longer slaves to him; we are no longer slaves to Satan. Just like the Israelites, we moved from death to life.

From the edge of the Red Sea, the nation of Israel headed toward the promised land, facing many challenges along the way. When they arrived at the Jordan River, Moses sent 12 spies into Canaan to scout out the land. When they returned, Joshua and Caleb were very excited and believed the land could be conquered. But the other 10 spies convinced the people of Israel that it was impossible. You know the rest of the story.

The Israelites were not willing to follow God's leadership, so He turned them back into the wilderness to wander for 40 more years until that generation died off. He finally allowed them to return to the bank of the Jordan River. This time, under the leadership of Joshua, they crossed over the Jordan River, and God gave them tremendous victory as they walked in obedience to Him.

Now, let us look at another similarity. Many people in the Church today have crossed over the Red Sea—salvation. They are saved. However, they have not crossed over the Jordan River—Lordship. Sadly, many believers in Christ are still wandering aimlessly in the wilderness when the victory is just on the other side of the Jordan—the promised land—if they would only surrender. The abundant life in Christ is our promised land. Many are saved and look forward to Heaven, but they have never become a part of the amazing journey on the way there.

It is truly sad to see so many believers who came to know Christ but have not found the joy of surrender or Lordship. They go to church, but they live a powerless life. All the while, it is within their grasp when they fully give their lives to Christ. Jesus calls us into the depths with Him. He calls children, students, and adults to lay down their lives so that He might give them life.

We cannot leave Lordship out of our teachings. To do so is to teach contrary to God's plan for the Church today. There is a cost, but we must explain that cost with joy, knowing that those who fully surrender to the Master will step into the abundant life. They will join with the Master as we work together to bring every tribe, nation, and tongue before the throne of God and the Lamb (Revelation 7:9).

We must help children understand that at salvation we crossed over from death to life. But new life comes when we lay down our lives to Christ—Lordship. Lordship is the starting point to abundant life. It is the path to righteousness. It is when we step out of the boat like Peter, in faith, and fully trust Christ with our lives. Then, and only then, do we offer God a sacrifice that is holy and pleasing in His sight (Romans 12:1).

Teaching Lordship

What I have found in teaching Lordship is there must be a call to action. Jesus used illustrations to teach spiritual truths. I have found that one of the most effective ways to call children to surrender is to ask them to move from one place to another. The Lord has used this powerfully throughout the last 18 years. Here are a few ways you can teach it to your preteens or students.

1. The Cross (Luke 9:23; Romans 12:1)

On multiple mission trips and retreats, I have laid down painter's tape on the floor in the shape of a very large cross. Then I invited children to lay down their lives in surrender to Christ by stepping into the outline of the cross. It is a powerful object lesson that quickly comes alive when they take action.

First and foremost, I have learned that I cannot call children to do something that I have not done myself. I found that if I am not allowing Christ to be Lord of my life, then this invitation, this calling of children, is a powerless message. This is a holy moment. Calling children to lay down their lives is holy and pleasing to God. Each time I have done this, the Spirit of God has moved differently and powerfully.

Before we begin the service, we have a time of worship. This is not a time for silly songs. It is a time of worship, so I would find songs that fit the moment of surrender. Worship prepares their hearts through prayer. The music plays so that they can hear it and worship along with it. Surrendering my own heart to the Lord and asking Him to fill me with His Spirit and to speak through me allows Him to do what He desires and not just what I desire.

The Word of God speaks for itself. It is unnecessary to go into a long message or exegetical breakdown of the passage of Scripture. I simply read the passage and encourage the children to respond in a spirit of worship. At this time, a song of surrender is usually played and then I invite them to come forward or to step out and sit in the cross on the floor. They are asked to sit down and bow their heads.

Madison Lowrie (former L.I.T.) shared,

> The first mission trip I ever went on was Jersey Village. It was so hot. I didn't know what to expect; I had never been away from home that long. The Lord spoke to brother Clint, and he put a cross on the ground with tape. He had us all stand on the outside of the cross and the Holy Spirit was there. It was tangible. That mission trip truly changed my life forever. Jersey Village is where it started for me.

2. Invitation to Step into the River

Another one of my favorite illustrations to use comes from Ezekiel 47:1-5. Ezekiel sees a vision of the temple of God. Water is flowing from the side of the temple. As the water flows out, it becomes deeper and deeper. Ezekiel is standing on the bank of the river when an angel takes a measuring line. He measures out thousand-cubit increments as the water goes deeper and deeper:

- ankle deep

- knee deep

- waist deep

- deep enough for swimming

To illustrate this in a worship service, I have used blue painter's tape to lay out an imaginary line or river in the front of the room. There is enough room for everyone in the room to step over the line "into the river" and sit down. This is a time of worship that leads them to a point of surrender. Again, Scripture speaks for itself. I read the Bible passage and then ask them where they are with God and where they want to be. "Are you on the bank? Ankle deep? Knee deep? Waist deep? Or are you swimming— all the way in with God? My invitation to you today is to give your all to the Lord, to go into the depths with Him. When we offer our lives fully to God, it is a holy and pleasing sacrifice to Him."

This, again, is a holy moment before the Lord. We take it very seriously and allow time for the Lord to minister to the children (as well as the adults). I usually continue to play soft worship music to help keep their minds focused on the Lord and what He is saying to them in the moment. I cannot tell you what the Lord might do, but you can never go wrong calling the children in your church to lay down their lives before the Lord. This will be a life-changing experience for them.

Marc Faulkenbery (adult) shared,

> You (Clint) did a really simple invitation. There weren't any emotional songs. There were songs playing. There was a simple invitation—it was simple. We bowed our heads to pray, and you asked kids to come up. I had my eyes closed, and I sort of looked up for a second. I thought, 'I will see which kids have gone down.' Everyone had gone down. Almost every child we had there had gone down to the front. As I looked at them, they were weeping.

They have emotions that they can't explain. They couldn't even explain it afterward. You know, that is the Holy Spirit working in their lives, and we don't fully understand it. To see them all up there, and they just didn't leave and were really broken. They were broken and in tears over their lives and over their sins. I believe the Holy Spirit really drove them there.

3. Step into the Basket—Hula Hoops

During one of our fall retreats with our preteens, I took along hula hoops. I remembered a story of a pastor of a small church in Mexico. At the end of the service, their tradition was to put a large basket for the offering in front of the pulpit at the front of the church.

At the end of the service, the people would walk to the front of the church and place their offering in the basket. The pastor looked back toward the rear of the church and saw an older gentleman standing and walking down the aisle. The man walked up and stepped into the large basket. The pastor was shocked! He asked the man, "What are you doing?" He said, "I have nothing to give but my life." He made a holy sacrifice pleasing to God. I told this story after our worship time. Holding a hula hoop in my hand, I said, "Boys and girls, I want to invite you to do something holy and pleasing for God. I invite you to take a hula hoop. This is like your basket. Take it outside, and if you are a ready and willing, step into it and sit down as an offering before the Lord. When you sit down, pray, 'Lord Jesus, I surrender. I give You my life as a living sacrifice.'" One by one, they came forward and grabbed their hula hoops, took them outside, and sat down in them in the courtyard.

I went outside a little later and saw them sitting in the hula hoops with their heads bowed. As I walked nearby, I could tell that the Lord had touched their lives at that moment. Many were in tears as the Lord revealed sin in their lives. It was a special moment. Again, it was that simple. I did not manipulate them with a hard message. I told them the story, read Romans 12:1, and invited them to respond. The Lord saw it as a holy moment, and they experienced His presence in a powerful way.

The Word of God Is the Word of God

Throughout my 33 years of ministry, I have seen the Word of God speak for itself. I truly believe if we do not believe what it says, we do not need to be ministering or working with children. God's Word has transformed my life, and it transforms the lives of children as they embrace God's calling. His calling is for all believers. Through His Word, we have spiritual encounters with the Master. From salvation, we move to a life of surrender and align our hearts with His mission—the Great Commission.

As an L.I.T., Will Isenblitter (L.I.T. 2015-21) was influenced by spending daily time in the Word of God. He shared,

> The most impactful aspect of this for me personally was the daily Bible studies that we had. They helped develop a habit that I have tried to carry through my entire life. My Bible study in the morning has and continues to ground me in the faith and keep a Godly perspective on the world rather than having a "what can I do today to further myself" type of attitude. My prayer is that the Lord will work in and through your life as you call the younger saints into the spiritual depths with the Father. I pray that you will step into the depths with Him and that you will find true joy as you come alongside the kids in your church to invite them deeper and deeper in their walk with Christ.

A Masking Tape Cross on a Church Floor by Madison Campbell Lowrie (L.I.T. 2004-2005)

L.I.T. is more than just a single chapter of my story; the ministry's impact is woven into the very tapestry of my entire life. The tagline of the ministry "empowering the next generation" is more than just a saying; it is a lifestyle, intertwined into the very DNA of all that is involved in the program. The founders believe and implement the truth that there is no such thing as a "junior" Holy Spirit, and because of that call-to-action and *their passion for His kingdom to come to Earth, my life has forever been changed.*

My salvation story began at an early age and was followed by water baptism shortly thereafter. However, the Spirit of God fell upon me and my fellow L.I.T. brothers and sisters during our mission trip to Jersey Village when we were baptized by the fire of the Holy Spirit. We all had the foundations of daily Bible reading, weekly discipleship, learning to fall in love with the Word of God, and memorizing critical verses all while becoming more and more emboldened in our faith. But that week, we encountered God in a way that can never be shaken or taken away from us. True repentance—complete and total mind shift—was the result. Our leaders listened to the prompting of the Holy Spirit and trusted Him, stepping into the unknown, and His kingdom flooded that place in a tangible manner.

Due to my foundation in L.I.T., I fall back on the simplicity of how a masking tape cross on a church floor ushered in the glory of God, and I remember the power of letting go and trusting Him. L.I.T. encouraged me to learn about God, taught me discipline in my studies, connected me with a community of believers, empowered me to share my faith in brave obedience, and led me to the cross. L.I.T. ushered me into the throne room and provided a space to encounter God that I will continue to carry throughout my days.

CHAPTER 6

Defining Discipleship

I must admit, when I started out moving toward discipling children, it was difficult to find a good definition. If you look at the church model today, are we making disciples who make disciples? Do we have a biblical model of discipleship when children are sequestered in the classroom where they hear the stories of the Bible but are not allowed to be a part of the story in the Church?

Discipleship is a duplication. Gallaty defines discipleship in this manner: "In essence, the D-Group is designed for the player to become a coach. Leaders must communicate this purpose at the outset of the group." 27 In other words, discipleship is when a leader duplicates himself in others. You might wonder if this is possible with children and preteens. The answer is yes. When we train and equip children, they can and will become disciple makers.

Discipled by Godly Women *by Grace Lehew (L.I.T. 2012-2013)*

I grew up in a Christian home and was heavily involved in my church for as long as I can remember. In 1st grade, I professed Jesus as my Lord and Savior. At such a young age, I did not realize what a blessing it was to be in a church that took discipling kids seriously. When I was in 4th grade, I started Leaders In Training. I was discipled by godly women, and I was taught how to serve and be a part of the Church. At 10 years old, I was entrusted with sharing the Gospel, studying the Bible, and living a life of obedience. I learned how to love the Church and love the lost.

Thus, I had a firm foundation in my life. There were many times when I failed to walk in obedience. For example, I lived in selfish ambition for most of the high school. I did a lot of great things for the Lord. However, I neglected the people I loved most. I was prideful, self-centered, and excluded people I loved. Because the Word was the foundation for my life, I did not stay in my sin. I had godly people who had been discipling me since I was 10 call me out in sin. As I read the Word, I was convicted of my actions. Because of that foundation, I could stand strong in the Lord.

L.I.T. set a pattern for the rest of my life. Currently, I am a student at Spurgeon College in Kansas City, seeking a degree in Intercultural Studies and International Church Planting with the hopes of training people to be missionaries. To this day, the Lord has been faithful to guide me, even in my own stubbornness. All glory be to Christ.

If I Can't Do It at Church, I Will Do It on My Own

Typically, children are receivers of information with very few opportunities to invest in the lives of others within the body of Christ. Some children naturally go out on their own and reach other children and disciple them on their own. Maggie returned from a mission trip in Oklahoma and felt burdened for her lost friends. She shared,

> *I saw my friends at school, and I knew that they needed the Lord. And so, I started a Bible study. I knew that I could do that because of the mission trip. Before I started L.I.T., I couldn't do anything. We prepared by doing stories and verses and things like that. So, I got comfortable and very confident that I could teach stories. So, I started a Bible study at school. I started out with three and now I have around seven girls coming. There are two girls that I led to Christ who are going to my Bible study—Jordan and Shelby. They are both sisters. I led Jordan before Shelby, which was on a Wednesday. I am very confident that I can lead them all to the Lord when they are ready.*

Those Kids Are Not Developmentally Ready to Do That

What I love is the shock and surprise I have seen in multiple leaders we have trained. They were going about their own business when they found out a kid in the church had started a Bible study at their school. They were surprised that the kids did not need their permission. They just did it. What happens when you begin to train children and have them serve in the church? They become confident that they can do anything for the Lord. This is so true for many children we have worked with. They do not need permission; they just do it. They want to serve, and when you make it possible for them to do so, they feel like they are part of the Church. It is key that your church become a platform for children to minister and serve alongside the adult leaders. They need a "Paul" in their lives to equip them to become Pauls themselves. The mentees become the mentors.

Teaching Versus Discipleship

Are we discipling children when we are using a developmental learning approach to teaching them in our churches? Can a child understand or embrace the heavier teachings of Scripture? If we are educating them and giving them a knowledge-based faith, then it might be a good idea to be aware of their developmental learning styles.

The truth is, we are not looking at a knowledge-based education in the church; we are looking at making disciples and developing the faith of children. Joel Rosenberg draws a wonderful comparison of teaching versus discipleship. The discipleship relationship is, "more personal, more practical, and more powerful." [28]

- A teacher shares information. A discipler shares his life.
- A teacher aims for the head. A discipler aims for the heart.
- A teacher measures knowledge. A discipler measures faith.
- A teacher is an authority. A discipler is a servant.
- A teacher says, "Listen to me." A discipler says, "Follow me." [29]

I challenged my disciple group leaders to invite preteens in their groups to help teach the Bible study on a regular basis. My goal was to have the preteens lead part of their group, giving them an opportunity that they otherwise would not have. To our surprise, the gift of teaching surfaced very quickly when they were released to lead. Micah Galey (L.I.T. 2008-2009) was in 5th grade when he began teaching in his small group. Through this process, he became an amazingly gifted teacher. As I recognized this, I continued to give him more and more opportunities to teach and disciple younger children. He shared,

> When I was in a discipleship class with Mr. Nigh, that was the first year I went and taught the younger kids. I believe it was a group of 2nd graders. That was the first time someone let me teach a class. I did it after stressing about it and freaking out about it for about a week. He thought I did so well that he made me...I mean let me... do it again and again and again. It rustrated me because I would stress about it so much. After a while, he looked at me and said, "Hey, you really have a gift for teaching."

Confidence to Disciple

As children and students are involved with ministry and missions, they develop the confidence to go out on their own. We have observed this on multiple occasions. Sandi St. Claire shared,

> I was frustrated at church and was about ready to quit. I decided I would meet with our preteens to see how they progressed in their discipleship. To my surprise, three of our preteens started Bible studies at their schools. They had already led multiple children to Christ. I could not believe it. They didn't need my help.

It will truly bless you is when you train children at your church and give them places to serve. They develop the confidence to do the same in the world. Shelby (5th grade) had a prayer rally at her school. They surrounded the flagpole in front of their school to pray for their school. What surprised everyone was this little 11-year-old girl standing in front of at least 50 children and adults and presenting the Gospel to them. Shelby has regularly been a part of the teaching team at her church.

Shelby now leads a weekly Bible study at her school. Here personal confidence as a teacher has soared to new levels. She recently taught at her church in front of hundreds of adults. She is an amazing, gifted young teacher. Fortunately for Shelby, her children's pastor provided a place for her serve and developed her gifts, which she uses to minister in her church.

This happens when teachers become disciplers. Instead of doing everything for the children, they come alongside them and give them opportunities to minister. The teachers know that they are not there to share knowledge but to model faith to the children they are leading. They model for the children, living out their faith in front of them. There is joy in seeing children struggling and their discipler standing beside them praying for them and encouraging them along their spiritual journey.

Joel had been serving in his church since he was in 5th grade. He regularly served and taught and went on mission trips with his church. He shared how God led him to start a Bible study:

> I have had the privilege of being on two mission trips. After I came home from the mission trip in Little Rock, Arkansas, it felt like God was calling me to not stop once I reached First Baptist Ozark and not let that die down. To carry it on at my school. As school started later that year, I decided I was going to start a Bible study at my school. I had to go to teachers to ask them if I could get into a classroom. Each one said no to me. Satan put up a lot of barriers to carry on what God wanted me to do. Eventually, I started the Bible study here at my church. It was a very successful thing. I believe that God was able to work through me and bring people to a knowledge of Him. It all stemmed off of that mission trip. L.I.T. has impacted my life. As you get into 5th and 6th grades, you go through L.I.T., and it really strengthens your foundation.

As I moved in the direction of children discipling younger children in my church, I realized that I had to set up some standards for our ministry to follow. Not every child is ready to disciple or mentor other kids. They had to be ready. So, our requirements were as follows:

1. They had to be believers. They could not teach something they did not have themselves.

2. They needed to be growing in their faith in Christ. We required them to be faithful in their personal quiet times and in their spiritual walk with Christ.

3. Christ was the Lord of their lives. We knew that they could not teach what they did not have or could not model.

4. They were not discipline problems at home, church, or school. I would regularly ask parents to report to me how their child was doing with regards to discipline issues.

They were recommended by their disciple group or ministry team leader. Having children disciple younger children had its challenges. We never allowed them to work with younger children on their own; they always had an adult leader present. However, the fruit was immediate. There was a positive peer pressure on both sides. Our preteens had to step it up. Looking back at being a 6th grader, Micah Galey (former L.I.T.) commented, "I realized that I was called to be a role model, so I had to take my faith seriously." On the other side, the younger children thought it was really cool to have older kids discipling them.

While I was walking down the hallway at church one Sunday, a little girl named Carly ran up to me and asked, "Have you seen Morgan?" Morgan was a 6th grader. I told Carly, "No." She ran upstairs to see if she could find Morgan there. Carly's mother walked up to me and said, "I think this is really amazing what you are doing. Carly loves Morgan. I love the fact that Morgan calls her every week to remind her to do her Bible study and to hear her memory verse." You light a fire in the hearts of kids, and they personally own the ministry you give them.

Those Who Have Not Been "Church-anized"

We led training with another local church. We taught the leaders there to allow the kids in their groups to lead each other. We taught them to move children incrementally from just sitting and listening to fully engaging them in their small groups. Here were the basic steps:

- I Do—You Watch
- I Do—You Help
- You Do—I Help
- You Do—I Watch
- You Do

To become a mentor-discipler, we must move children deeper and deeper into the depths with God. This was truly key to their faith development and developing confidence to minister. The church is one place where a person can fail and we will stand alongside them until they succeed.

Mike and Cari taught 3rd-grade girls in small groups at their church. They were new believers by about three years. They had not been "church-anized," meaning they did not grow up in the church. They went through the training and immediately started letting their girls lead their group. They did not know any different. By the end of their second year, their girls were leading the entire time. They could not wait to have their turn at teaching. Mike sent me a picture of a little girl standing in front of her small group teaching and the other girls raising their hands to answer a question.

I taught these same concepts with the leaders at my church for years. One year during the spring semester, I decided to review the steps to the process with our leaders. I walked through them step-by-step and told the leaders that it was about now that their kids should be leading their groups. Shortly afterward, one of my best teachers stopped me in the hallway and said, "Clint, I have truly blown it this semester. I knew better. I have been lecturing my girls every week and not allowing them to take part in leading each other."

Why should we want children to teach and lead out? Why is this so important? Ownership! They own the ministry that they are a part of. That does not come about from them simply observing but through doing. This is when ministry gets exciting. This model of ministry can be overwhelming, but the fruits are tremendous. Right before your eyes, God will raise up powerful leaders in your midst.

Lecturing vs. Teaching

While I was working on my dissertation, I was also tackling a problem in my church and for other churches. How can we transition preteens into student ministry? I won't go into the full details of my situation, but the question was, how do we continue a leadership development process in the church as the preteens move from the children's ministry into the student ministry? What needed to take place for this to happen successfully?

Nine new 7th-graders were eager to work with me on my project. Each one of them took a spiritual gift test and then was assigned to a ministry position in my church under a mentor. They were also required to do a daily quiet time for six weeks. The kids loved it. They would serve in the church during the first hour on Sunday morning, and then we would meet afterwards to debrief.

During our first debriefing, I asked them how they felt about serving in our church on Sunday morning. Their answers might surprise you: "I felt like I was a part of the Church for the first time." "I just sat and observed before. Now I feel like what I am doing is important." Most of them gave a similar response to my question. They felt like they were finally a part of the body of Christ.

In our fourth meeting together, we had another discussion about them serving and how they felt afterward. It was apparent that they were building new confidence and a newfound joy in serving in the church. Timothy (12 years old) looked at me during the meeting and said, "Four weeks ago, I was sitting in a Bible study here at church. I don't remember anything that was said that day or the weeks before." What was truly sad to me was that he was in class with a teacher that I thought was one of my best. The problem: the teacher was a lecturer.

What I learned from this project was noteworthy:

- We should not stop the process of training students to walk with Christ daily.
- They need to have strong accountability to grow in their faith.
- They hold on to their faith when they continue to serve in the church using their gifts to build up the body of Christ.

"Kids Should Not Be Serving Until They Are 18"

As I mentioned earlier, I did a study in my church. It was truly a joy to watch these kids excel. However, this did not come about without some resistance. Three of our new 7th graders were helping teach in our preschool, and I thought we were moving along at a great pace...until I got lectured. When I walked up to the door of a preschool room where our students were assisting, the teacher stepped out into the hallway with me and said, "I do not agree with this. My dad was a pastor, and he did not believe any child should be serving until they turned 18."

The problem with this type of thinking is that it devalues children. Children have a calling from the Lord, and we must embrace their calling to ministry in the church and the world. We must provide them with a platform to minister. That way we are being obedient to Paul's call to equip the saints (including the younger saints) "for the work of ministry" (Ephesians 4:11-13).

Have you ever been prepared to teach a lesson and then found yourself saying, "Lord, I can't do this without You"? Maybe you start teaching or sharing and you just do not have the Spirit's power. You find yourself praying in your heart, giving the Holy Spirit control, and then you end up teaching beyond what you prepared. You are overjoyed when you finish because the Holy Spirit spoke through you.

This is how it is for children, too! When they have an opportunity to teach or lead, they are faced with the same sentiments. "Do I do it myself, or do I ask God to do it through me?" They experience the same power that we do as adults but in different ways—it is the same Holy Spirit that moves through them. Think about this for a moment: If they experience the Holy Spirit just as we do, then we need to give them opportunities to serve using their gifts from Him.

Having children sit and listen to you teach them is one thing, but I challenge you the next time you are in class with them to say, "Next week, I want you to teach this part of the lesson." That will be a game-changer for them. Do not just make it a one-time thing but an ongoing plan if you want to help them develop their gifts and experience God working through them. Timothy in the Bible had Paul in his life to disciple and equip him; however, there came a time when Timothy was charged by Paul to lead out and do it on his own. Timothy had a godly mother and grandmother, but it was Paul and the Church that equipped him to minister using his spiritual gifts.

Make this a part of your DNA as a teacher, leader, and/or administrator. Kids will connect more powerfully with God while in the midst of doing ministry. As you walk alongside them and allow them to minister using their gifts in the power of the Holy Spirit, they experience God's presence and become firm in their faith.

You must ask yourself, "Do I want to be a discipler or a teacher?" Do I want to model my faith and call children to come alongside me? There is education, and there is discipleship. Putman says, 'Many pastors believe they are making disciples by preaching sermons that teach their congregation what the Bible says. They see discipleship as simply a transfer of knowledge from teacher to student, and the result will be a changed life."[30] The same is true for numerous teachers today. They are not willing to take the extra time their group needs to go to next level discipleship. They want to teach their group; however, they do not want to take the time to allow their group to join them in ministry together. Philippians 2:22 (NIV) says, "But you know that Timothy has proved himself, because as a son with his father he has served with me in the work of the gospel."

A Start in Children's Ministry *by Breanne Morgan Galey (L.I.T. 2009-2010)*

For a long time, I felt like I didn't have potential. I felt like I was just a kid. I couldn't do anything, and I started to get really, really discouraged. I wanted to teach. I thought it would be so cool to help other kids. When I went to Ms. Tricia and asked her, "Can I go help with the younger kids' class?" she said, "Sure, let's do it!" She got really excited!

And so, me and my friend Hannah started teaching (when we were) in 5th grade. We went into a 2nd-grade class, and we got to assist. And that was, to me, that was a really big deal because someone cared about me. Someone said you are enough, you can do this, and they didn't look down on me like I was a kid, like I couldn't do it. They believed in me even though I didn't have a seminary degree. And even though I hadn't been trained in it all my life, I went and started assisting, and I was only 10 years old.

After about two months, the teachers in that class were called to move, and they were gone in one week. We had no notice, so my friend Hannah and I started teaching, and we had an hour and a half with about ten crazy little 2nd graders. And we, well as Mr. Clint always says, we were thrown into the deep end. We just had to learn how to do it, and no one said, "You're not an adult. You can't do that." They just let us teach, and we were able to gain so much experience through just interacting with them, trying to get over all those problems and hard things. So that was a really big start to my journey, a start in children's ministry.

(Breanne and Hannah taught until they graduated from high school.)

CHAPTER 7

Children and the Holy Spirit

When speaking of the Holy Spirit and His role in the life of the child, it is quite amazing to behold. I wrote earlier about my initial preteen mission trip when, for the first time, I heard a young man share how he felt the presence of God. He said to me, "When I shared today, there was something like fire going through me." This was an 11-year-old boy. In my years of ministry up to that point, I had never seen or heard anything like this. It compelled me at the time to document and record what I was seeing.

It is quite incredible to witness how the Spirit of God works in and through children. They do not understand it, but they feel His presence in ways that are unexplainable to them. Channing (6th grade) shared, "It's amazing. I can, like, feel God's presence. I get goosebumps. Sometimes, I don't know what I am saying."

When reading Acts 1:8 in the past, I never considered children in this context. But it is absolutely true that the Spirit works through them, just as He works through adults. "But you will receive power when the Holy Spirit has come upon you; and you shall be My witnesses." What they experience is supernatural. When you see it firsthand, you will know it is undeniable.

In this chapter, we will look at the observations and impressions of many of the adult leaders on the mission trips. These observations show many consistent markers.

1. Children become bold prayer warriors for the lost.

2. The Holy Spirit moves and speaks through them.

3. When the Holy Spirit takes over, He speaks through them, and they have no recollection of what they shared.

4. They sense His presence in their lives.

5. They become sensitive to the Holy Spirit's leading.

6. They become fearless in sharing their faith.

7. They experience inexpressible joy after the Spirit works through them.

8. There is a rapid spiritual growth that occurs in ministry and missions.

9. Their spiritual gifts manifest very quickly in ministry and missions.

10. They become in tune with God and His heart for the lost in the world.

The Holy Spirit Moves and Speaks Through Children

For children and preteens, it is apparent the Holy Spirit takes over at some point and speaks through them. Jesus told us, "Whatever is given you in that hour, speak that; for it is not you who speak, but the Holy Spirit" (Mark 13:11b). This verse comes true in the lives of children. When they cry out to God, the Spirit of God takes over and speaks. As you read the following quotes from multiple children and preteens, look at them in the context of Mark 13:11b. What is remarkable is these testimonies span over the last 16 years, and they are very consistent across the board.

Sarah (5th grade) was on a mission trip in San Marcos, Texas. On this trip, several of our team members became ill. Because of this situation there was a shortage of leadership. Sarah had personal fears to overcome, but through this experience, she felt God speak through her. She shared, "Once we started preaching, at that time I was just shaking. I remember praying to myself and saying, 'God, I cannot do this by myself. This is all you.' I remember going brain dead at that point. I still to this day do not know exactly what I said. I just knew that He had given me a calling to go and teach."

Holland was in 6th grade. We saw tremendous potential for the gifts the Lord had given him. I asked him on many occasions to teach at events for our ministry. We were invited to a preteen camp one summer to lead an event, and I asked Holland to share the Gospel that evening. He stood on stage in front of 700 preteens and leaders and shared the message. Ten preteens accepted Christ that night. "I was praying to God, and I said, 'God, just give me the strength and courage to go do this.' When I got up there, I just kind of let the words go."

At one of the ministry sites during a mission trip, Jordan (6th grade) was asked to share his testimony. Jordan shared, "It was really great. I went up there today and did my testimony. I was scared stiff. I said, 'Oh God, please help me.' I said something that I don't have any idea what I said. But God spoke through me, and I still don't know what I said."

There are many opportunities to witness to people on a mission trip or community outreach. These events give preteens chances to share their faith and counsel lost children. These opportunities allow preteens the ability to practice what they have learned in their churches. Haylee shared, "When I witnessed to these children today, there was this amazing sensation running through me. I was about to cry." She felt the Spirit's presence in a powerful way. There is always the fear, but when the Lord works, they can do amazing things for Him.

Sarah was a shy 5th grader. It was very challenging for her to stand up and teach during our preteen mission trips. The thought of standing in front of a group of kids was terrifying to her. Out of fear, she cried out to God, and He answered. She shared, "Today, I was going to teach the red page. I was thinking, 'God, I don't think I can do this. Please speak through me.' By the time it was all over, I had no clue what I said."

As I mentioned earlier, Carilyn worked with us at the church doing administrative tasks when she was as young as 9 years of age. God took her to an all-new level by calling her to teach during a mission trip. Even as a teen, it was very difficult for her to speak in front of a group of people. She was definitely a behind-the-scenes person. She shared,

"God spoke through me today, and I don't remember what I said. I got up to share my testimony and my mind went blank."

Joshua was a particularly quiet 6th grader. It was very uncommon for him to want to be in front of anyone. He was so shy and timid. On the outside, you probably would not pick him to teach or lead out, but God had a greater plan. Joshua spoke in front of about 200 people during an outreach event during a mission trip. Joshua shared, "I knew God was speaking through me. Even though I stopped for that little period of time, I was like, I took a deep breath, and I said, 'God, take over,' and He went through me. He spoke through me."

Makenzie was asked to teach during a large outreach event. She had about three hours to prepare to teach the Wordless Book. She practiced and practiced and still did not feel ready. Then when the time to teach arrived, she walked up on the stand, and God moved through her. She shared,

> So, I get up on stage, and I was about to talk. The Holy Spirit just kind of poured out on me, and I don't really know what I said at all. But ah, it was completely and totally not me. It was the Holy Spirit. If the Holy Spirit did not do that, I am pretty sure it would have been a disaster. I just felt that was really cool how the Holy Spirit really helped me through it.

Pressley was asked to teach during a summer mission trip to Waxahachie, Texas. I had asked her to teach because she had been teaching children's worship and younger children at her church. She was an amazingly gifted teacher, and she was only in 5th grade. We did not expect that Pressley would completely amaze us with her gift on the mission trip. She had such a powerful presence on the stage that you would not have thought she was a kid. She was fantastic. She felt the Spirit's presence in her life that evening as she taught in front of about 200 children and adults. Pressley shared, "As I was teaching, the Holy Spirit was moving through me."

One of the most common statements from children and preteens on mission trips is, "God spoke through me today, and I do not know what I said." We have heard this same statement so many times on the multitude of mission trips we have done. It is a simple description of a powerful work of God in and through a child's life. They just do not know how to describe what they are experiencing, but they know it was God—the Holy Spirit—who did it.

Through personal observation and various interviews and testimonies, it is clear to me that the Holy Spirit moves and speaks through children. One parent shared, "When the leaders got out of the way, the Holy Spirit moved powerfully through our kids." This is a common response to what they experience. From numerous observations, I have learned that the Holy Spirit takes control for a moment of time and speaks through them. They are aware, but there seems to be a disconnect for that instant as He speaks through them.

The Hindrance to the Work of the Holy Spirit

I never thought of myself hindering the work of the Holy Spirit in children in my church. I did what everyone else was doing. I found the best resources, and I trained my teachers. We taught the children about missions and missionaries around the world. I took them to what I thought were the best children's and preteen camps, and I witnessed the Lord speaking to their hearts. I was committed to doing the best I could to raise up spiritual champions in my church. But now I realize there is a missing piece to the puzzle—missions and ministry.

Sadly, our structure of church and ministry for kids is pretty much the same across the board. Children are spectators and recipients of knowledge where there is no ready way for them to put their faith into action in the body of Christ. They are not allowed to minister—not because we do not want them to, but because there are no places made available for them to do so.

Could it be that, in all our busyness, we have jumped off track from the Great Commission?

What we have witnessed is that the Holy Spirit shows up in powerful ways on the mission trips and outside the church. The goal of the Church is to equip the saints for the works of ministry. That ministry must move from inside the church building out into the community and the world.

Not Enough Places for the Spiritual Gifts of Children

There just are not enough places for all the gifts of the church to be used. This is especially true for our kids. We have observed, however, the Holy Spirit's movement in the lives of preteens in powerful ways on mission trips and in community ministry. Peter tells us that everyone has received a gift or gifts. "As each one has received a gift, minister it to one another, as good stewards of the manifold grace of God" (1 Peter 4:10).

What surprised me was the spiritual gifts of children and how they would manifest as we involved them in ministry. They were allowed to teach or lead in my church. It was during ministry that their spiritual gift(s) would manifest, and my observation confirmed it. I read in Scripture that they had gifts, but seeing them firsthand really caught my attention...and somewhat caught me off guard.

Children Are Not the Target of our Ministry

The unique point we are missing here is that children are a gift to the body of Christ. They are not the target of our ministry; they are joint members of the body of Christ. Leaders many times will be amazed at what they witness. It is a matter of releasing them to minister and stepping back and supporting them as they serve.

Adults Are Surprised by What They Witness

We have worked with multiple churches and hundreds of leaders. I love it when adults see for themselves the Holy Spirit's gifting of children. It completely at times catches them by surprise.

Time and again, when adults witness firsthand God moving through a child, they are truly shocked by what they see. Laura was on our third mission trip to Pineville. She shared in tears on a Friday evening what she had observed: "To see our kids just shine up there and do the things they do. A lot of people don't do this. I mean, they are 5th and 6th graders. They got up there and did everything. Neile was great. To watch her get up there and teach the Wordless Book was just amazing. I have only known Neile for just over a year, and she has come out of her box."

Janice (adult leader) had the same experience. She was truly stunned by what she observed: "I have never been on a trip. I was really scared. My life is blessed, and my life is changed…from each and every one of you, from our kids, and from watching kids teach kids." Janice saw the Holy Spirit manifest in the lives of preteens in her group. It is hard to describe what you see because it is so powerful when God speaks through children.

Many adults go on our mission trips thinking they are going to teach the preteens and disciple them during the week. What truly happens is they end up learning from the children. Lorinda Bodiford shared, "I started teaching the kids a year ago thinking I was going to teach the kids. Isn't it strange when the children teach you? These kids have no fear. They aren't ashamed." Bruce Coleman shared, "I was on this trip to show the kids how to do everything. What I didn't expect was that they taught me."

Katlyn had been on multiple mission trips as a preteen. As a student, she went on our mission trip to Sapulpa, Oklahoma. During the trip, she went out with a group of preteens to a ministry site. As she watched the kids minister, she was truly blessed by what she observed. She shared, "And I just want you guys to know that you are amazing. Most of the adults in the world would not think of doing this. They are scared. I know that some of you guys are too, but you just push through it."

Amber watched in amazement as a young 5th grader, Kara, witnessed to an elderly gentleman at their ministry site. Kara was not going to give up on him. Amber shared, "I am truly blown away by what these kids are capable of doing. There is no word to describe how amazing it is to see a little girl try to lead someone in the way of salvation and do it in such a great way. It's all God. It's amazing." Kara quoted verse after verse. When the man did not respond to her, she went outside the house for a moment and cried out to God for the man's salvation.

Jerry attended our San Marcos mission trip. He was truly disturbed because of what he observed on the trip. He shared,

> And then I realized that through all of this that I was just a big coward. And I know that there are more of us sitting out there. That night, these kids had moved me so much that I was sitting at the back of the church as usual. The song 'I will never be ashamed of You' (by Hillsong) just hit me. A lot of times I have been just a big coward. I was selectively sharing, and these kids were saying, 'Mr. Jerry, just stand right there, and we will go out and share.' Even when it came to sharing…they were all over it.

Kim was a new believer. She had never been on a mission trip; this was her first. When she went out with kids, she knew something was different about them. They were doing things that she had never done herself. She shared, "My kids showed me that they knew more than I ever knew about God. They reached out to those kids and showed them love and mercy."

The Church Is the Training Ground—Missions Is the Practicum

Keri Meek from Hillcrest Baptist Church shared, "We take kids on mission trips every summer. Every year, I have parents come to me and ask. 'If you had to choose between camp and the mission trip, which would you suggest?' Hands down, I say, 'Send the kids on the mission trip instead of camp.'" Keri shared her experience when taking children off-campus from her church on a mission trip:

On the mission trip, the focus is not on the kids, not on themselves. It is an outward expression of their faith. You cannot reproduce what happens on a mission trip here where they live. It gets them out of their comfort zones. It gets them into the deep waters. They must have total reliance on the Holy Spirit.

If you have ever been on a mission trip, you know that some of the days are hard. You experience situations you are not used to being in. We can't do it on our own; we must constantly seek the Lord. That's something you can't teach a child from a book or in a classroom setting. They have to experience the power of the Holy Spirit helping them and guiding them through situations.

The kids actually lead everything on the mission trip. They have been developing the spiritual disciplines all year long. They are spiritually prepared because of everything we have been teaching them. They are understanding who they are in Christ. It's like a practicum. They are taking it out and exercising all of those things.

Keri's observations are so true. The church is the training ground, whereas the mission trip is the "practicum." The point is, we train them and then take them out. That is what God is calling us to do (Ephesians 4:11-14). That is when true joy begins in your ministry because there is great fruit from all your hard labor. My goal every year at my church was to start off discipling and training our preteens in our church, and by March, we were out in the community ministering together.

Children Become Sensitive to the Holy Spirit

It is a joy to watch children as they learn to hear the voice of God—the Holy Spirit. They can sense Him speaking to their hearts. I have become intentional in training leaders to allow children to listen to the Spirit and see what He guides them to do. We all have been blessed by stepping back and letting the Lord work.

One of our assignments on the mission trip was to encourage the preteens to pray and step back and watch what the Holy Spirit led them to do. One of our groups in Willow Park, Texas, went out to a local apartment complex. Upon arrival, the leaders asked the preteens what they should do. They talked and prayed, and then they went out to pray. They walked to each apartment door, laid their hands on it, and prayed.

Elizabeth (5th grade) shared, "When we laid our hands on the door, everything went silent. You couldn't hear anything, just us praying." Elizabeth's mother, who was standing nearby, shared what she personally witnessed:

> We watched as the kids moved from door to door praying. They also stopped and prayed in the stairwells. Every time they touched the doors or stairwells and started praying, you could not hear anything—it was dead silence. I asked them what they were praying about when they laid hands on the doors and in the stairwells. They said that the people inside the apartment would feel God's presence. When they went down the stairs, we prayed the same.

Sandi St. Claire shared,

> At one door, they heard a baby crying and a woman screaming. They prayed, and the crying and screaming stopped. Right then, the lady walked out the door. She asked them, 'What are you doing?' They said, 'We prayed for you.' The woman immediately broke down in tears and said, 'Thank you! I really needed it.' Then the kids became even bolder. They went to the playground and prayed over every toy. They said that when they prayed, 'the world stopped.' Because of what happened to them, they are still on fire for the Lord today... three years later...because of what happened to them.

There are times when you do not have to say a word. They know the Lord's still small voice, and they listen and obey. Jennifer Smith shared that when her daughter went on the mission trip, she really sensed God telling her to speak to the kids. She had such a love for them—that was the Holy Spirit working in her life. What a joy it has been watching the Holy Spirit work!

Sometimes, we absolutely must get out of the way and allow the Spirit to work. The kids do not need us to hold their hands—they can take hold of the Master's hand and allow Him to guide them. Darci Page (parent) shared, "I enjoyed the mission trip last summer. One of the blessings I received from that was just watching when the adults got out of the way what God would do through those kids."

Rapid Spiritual Growth Through Ministry and Missions

One development we have noticed in the lives of preteens on mission trips and during community ministry is the level of growth they experience within a very short time from God working in their lives. When given the opportunity to minister using their gifts, they very quickly excel to new levels and spiritual heights. This has been witnessed by multiple church leaders.

Marc was from a church near Houston. He knew the 6th graders on the trip because he was their Sunday school teacher. What he did not expect was the rapid spiritual growth of those kids he worked with. He shared, "We know the level of their maturity and where they are at, and we have seen them go beyond that really rapidly here, which could only be God working in their lives. We have also seen the movement of the Holy Spirit."

When children have the freedom to minister, it certainly blesses those who see. The preteens quickly move to new levels of maturity. Brandi Raines shared, "I really saw a lot of the kids step up and lead, and I definitely saw many grow in their walk with Christ." Jamie Brown from Springfield, Missouri, witnessed her preteens change before her eyes. She shared, "In the course of one week, the fear and timidity of our L.I.T.s' spirits were replaced with readiness and eagerness."

It is hard to understand, but kids grow very rapidly in the midst of ministry. They move to a new level of confidence in ministry. Clint Lawson shared his observation: "I saw my preteens grow up spiritually right before my eyes." Cynthia said, "I saw a boldness increase in several students. Some of our students had 'lightbulb' moments about what missions is really about. It is a confirmation that they can lead and are called to it now."

Leaders witness firsthand the work of the Holy Spirit in the lives of their kids. You just cannot question it when you see it for yourself. Catherine shared, "I saw my students grow in confidence, awareness of the presence and work of the Holy Spirit, and the assurance of their salvation." Tammie witnessed this personally on the mission trip she attended: "I saw the joy in the kids full of the Spirit. Even during 'chores,' they were laughing and enjoying working for the Lord and being filled with the Holy Spirit."

Another observation is a new boldness that occurs in our preteens. During the first few days on a mission trip, they are fearful. By the end of the week, they are fearless. Their personal confidence builds every day to a point of celebration of what God did through them. Amy shared, "He (God) gave the kids boldness to speak—some didn't want to do anything on Monday, but later in the week were excited to speak."

Children become the hands and feet of Jesus as the Holy Spirit ministers through them. They love children with great compassion, which proves the work of the Holy Spirit flowing through their lives. They grow a love for the lost world and become passionate about joining God on His mission.

The Holy Spirit Is in Them—We Only Need to Release Them to Minister

As we have discussed in this chapter, the Holy Spirit moves and speaks in the lives of children. They do not fully understand it, but they know that God can use them to share His love and the truth of His Word. Their gifts are present, but many times, they will not discover their spiritual gifts until they are allowed to minister.

Sherry York from Northview Baptist Church shared,

I have sat back and listened to what has come out of the mouths of some of those kids when they are teaching and leading worship and doing some of those things. And I sit there and say, 'Wow! Did I just hear what I heard? Did I really hear the prayer they just prayed?' Or, 'Did I just hear them pray Scripture that they have learned and then be able to apply that Scripture?' It has been an awesome experience.

It may be hard to comprehend what you have read in this chapter. The Lord is working in powerful ways in our children and students today. I pray that your heart has been stirred to action and that you will seek the Lord for a vision for your ministry to release this generation of world changers in your church, your community, and the world.

This message came from a 12-year-old boy named Jordan. It was on a Thursday evening of our mission trip. Each evening we had testimony times where our preteens and leaders were encouraged to testify about their experiences. After Jordan got up to the microphone, it was very apparent that the Spirit of God was speaking through him. When he stepped down from the stage, there was not a dry eye on any of the adults' faces. Jordan shared,

First off, I want y'all to give a standing applause to God right now. Stand up. (All the children and leaders stood and applauded and whooped.)

It made me feel pretty good to be able to speak to these kids, and I'm sure it made y'all feel pretty good, too? How many of y'all got a little uncomfortable with what y'all were doing, like you weren't really used to it? You know, like that? Well, it paid off, didn't it? 70 new recruits, 70 new people to the army of God, 70 new people to the family of Christ. (More applause and whooping) *Well, some of y'all may think that it was a little hard, some of y'all already know that was God doing this.*

It's amazing to me, just completely amazing, that even though Jesus is perfect, He never did anything wrong. He was accused of many wrongdoings and had to hang on the cross with two criminals. He had to go through 9 hours of suffering in pain, 9 hours of mockery, because He loved us. And even when He shouted out, 'My God, My God, why are You forsaking me?' and they asked Him (if He wanted) some painkiller-type stuff, He didn't take it because He wanted to go in it all for us. Just for us. And after those 9 hours, He shouts out, 'IT IS FINISHED,' and then dies on the cross. But then the stone was removed, and He had arisen three days later. And when He did this, He created a bridge from Earth to Heaven to let us escape from sin and all of its horrors to go to Heaven and all of its glories. He did this because He loves us. And out of all that He did for us, all those miracles, all we had to do was open the door to our hearts and let Him in. And when He did this, He opened the gateway to Heaven to let us in.

Whenever I look at that picture (pointing to a picture in the stained-glass windows), like I did today—that picture over there that says, 'My beloved Son'—today, when I first came in here, that was the only picture that was shining really brightly. God did all these miracles for us. He spoke through us to those kids. He did all this for us just because He loves us. Out of all the universe He created—all the planets, all the stars, the sun, the solar system, the galaxies— He comes down, and He sees me. He sees us—some puny little things that He created, and out of all He made, all these glories, He comes and sees us because He loves us. And that means more to me than anything ever. It's amazing.

L.I.T. Shaped My Spiritual Life Tremendously *by Ketnarly Estimon*
(L.I.T. 2004-2005)

As a young girl, L.I.T. shaped my spiritual life tremendously! The key components were identity, leadership, and discipleship. I was taught my identity as a daughter and co-heir of Christ, and this life-transforming truth has made me the woman I am today. Through discipleship, I learned what it meant to live a life of integrity while following Jesus.

The discipline of quiet time or daily fellowship with God was impressed in my heart. I was encouraged to memorize scriptures that I can recite to this day. One of my favorites is Psalm 119:11 — "I have hidden your word in my heart that I might not sin against you." The scriptures and truths I learned in L.I.T. have stuck with me and have been an anchor throughout my life. It is said that leadership is caught, not taught. I am grateful that at a young age, I was not just told that I am a leader, but I was actually given leadership positions through L.I.T. By way of serving, I learned how to lead on my knees while giving God all the glory. This has not been lost on me in my adult life. I have gone on to serve in college ministry, mission trips, and even in my job as a nurse. It is no small thing to give the gift of the Gospel to a child and tell them to share it with the world. I am forever grateful that L.I.T. gave me such a gift. May God be glorified!!

CHAPTER 8

Children and Prayer

"For though we walk in the flesh, we do not war according to the flesh. For the weapons of our warfare are not carnal but mighty in God for pulling down strongholds, casting down arguments and every high thing that exalts itself against the knowledge of God, bringing every thought into captivity to the obedience of Christ, and being ready to punish all disobedience when your obedience is fulfilled." (2 Corinthians 10:3-6)

As I write this chapter, I testify as one who has personally witnessed some amazing things when children pray. You might be thinking that children just pray "cat and dog" prayers. But when you sit in their midst and hear them crying out to God, you know that they feel God's presence in very powerful ways. Many of us have witnessed that they are different.

They go further into the depths of prayer than many adults. I always encourage adults on our mission trips to sit with them, especially during their prayer times. I tell them, "Just sit and listen to them pray." Lorinda shared, "If you could picture boys and girls laying hands on each other and praying and adults sitting back with their mouths open. That was a little bit of what I saw. I saw kids pray in ways that I have not seen adults, and I was astounded."

They Have an Encounter with a Holy God (Isaiah 6:1-8)

They sense God's presence so powerfully at times that they are broken over personal sins in their lives. The Lord also speaks to them in incredible ways. Jonathan (5th grade) shared,

When we were at the altar praying, God gave me a wake-up call that is going to totally change my life. God made me realize that I was a sunbathing Christian enjoying the fact that I may go to Heaven and at the same time not going to the water of God's grace. He told me that it is not going to be as good if you don't go into the water.

Children sense the Lord's presence in special ways. They, like Isaiah, realize that they are sinners in the presence of a Holy God. It is a beautiful picture, not one of condemnation but of a desire to have their hearts right before God. Tate shared, "This week God revealed a lot of sin in my life. When we were praying, I did not realize I had that much sin. So, I had to repent a lot and ask a lot of people for forgiveness."

Once they make the connection with God, their hearts are set on fire with a passion to sit at the feet of the Father. Brittany shared, "This week when we were praying and everything, God made me realize that I was judging people when I got here this week. God laid on my heart that I should go to this person and ask forgiveness."

I remember a mother on our trip comforting her daughter who was sitting on the floor weeping. She felt the Spirit's presence so powerfully that she wept in His presence. Her mother told her, "Honey, that is the Holy Spirit you are feeling. It is hard to explain God's presence." She just sat there on the floor, and the Lord was ministering to her in a powerful way. One of our kids, Elijah, was sharing on stage and said, "What was amazing was one of my friends was up here crying. I didn't expect it. He was just sobbing for Jesus. I asked him what was up, and he said, 'I realized how much God loves me.'"

They Become Empowered Intercessors

It is hard to explain why, but after their brokenness over sin, they quickly move to interceding for the lost. This is especially true on mission trips. It becomes personal as they realize God's tremendous love for them in a new and fresh way. They turn that fresh revelation into a passion for the lost.

Victoria (adult) shared, "I have seen kids pray for hours just for the kids they have seen that day, the kids they were ministering to and talking to who were lost. It honestly moved me. I did not know that kids could do anything like that. I have grown up in a church, and I have never experienced anything like this. My youth group has never done that. It is like a match that lit a fire."

God Speaks to Them in Special Ways

During our mission trips, we pray for the nations of the 10/40 Window. It is a moving time for children when they see that there are so many lost people in that region of the world. Tyler (6th grade) shared, "When we were praying for all these countries last night, I asked myself, 'Why do these countries have to be like this?' I felt God speak to me, and I felt like He said that He made these countries like they are because He wanted people like us to go and share the Gospel whenever and wherever."

Teaching Children How to Pray

There is an old saying, "Faith is caught not taught." You can talk about prayer, but when you pray with children, they learn. LaJuana Ross (youth leader) approached me one Sunday morning and hugged my neck. She shared, "Clint, I have been teaching 7th grade girls for over 40 years. This group of girls that just moved up into my class are prayer warriors." Her husband Richard shared, "We had a group of girls over to our house. They had a prayer time. They started praying, and we had to stop them to eat dinner. They said, 'It didn't feel like we even prayed that long.'"

God Reveals Himself to Them in Different Ways

We were interviewing children the week of our 2015 mission trip. Brooke (5th grade) was from a church near Houston. Her leader approached me and said, "You have to hear Brooke's story."

On the Monday evening of our Granbury, Texas, mission trip, Brooke accepted Christ. But her story is very different than most. She shared,

It was Monday night, and you (Clint) called and said, "If you want to surrender your life to Jesus, you can come up and kneel at the stage," and a bunch of people did that, and we were all like crying and praying and stuff like that. Then I had a vision while we were praying and listening to the music.

You know how we all have pictures in our minds, how we picture stories in the Bible. Well, I had the picture in my mind of Jesus walking on water, except no one else was walking with Him. I was like under the water, and then He pulled me out. So, I accepted Him then. I felt like He was pulling me out of the water and saying, "You are fine now; you are with Me. You can walk on water with Me."

As I said earlier, some things cannot be explained. When she shared her story with me, I rejoiced that the Lord gave her such a vivid picture in her mind. Her vision was very powerful. That is something that I do not believe she will ever forget.

Spiritual Warfare

We have observed children who move quickly into spiritual warfare when reaching out to the lost. They quickly are attuned to the situation and many times their prayers intensify for the person they are witnessing to. Kara (5th grade) attended our Ozark, Missouri, mission trip. She and one of her leaders visited an older gentleman at an apartment complex who did not know Christ. She shared,

> I went outside and started crying. My friend said to stop crying, and I said, "No, there is a war going on in there, and Satan is not going to win. This little old man is not going to hell; he is going to Heaven." I went back into the house, and he asked me what I was doing out there. I told him that I was praying for him. I told him I wanted to see him on the day of judgment when Jesus brings His kids back home. I want to see him at those gates. I want to see him smiling, and I want to see him excited that he did make the decision in his life. I told him, "I want you to accept Christ."

There are obvious distractions that happen at different ministry locations that are out of our control. However, the kids would sometimes pray, and God would quickly answer and remedy the problem. Kiya shared, "For the past few days at our site there has been like construction going on, and it was really loud. We had been asking for it to go away so that it did not become a distraction. So today, they showed up for about 20 minutes, and then they left. They didn't come back the rest of the time we were at our site. I believe God answered our prayers."

We have taken children into many government housing projects or low-income areas. On multiple occasions, fights would break out or there were conflicts between residents there. Jenny shared, "Today at our site, there were adults fighting and screaming really loud and saying bad words. We got together and prayed, and it stopped."

Sometimes, we have ideas and do not have the supplies we need for a certain ministry opportunity. Some prayers seem so simple, but to a loving Heavenly Father, He provides. Kaylee (5th grade) shared, "Today, we were needing beach balls to play a game at our site. We prayed that we could get some beach balls. As we rode to our site, we turned the corner, and sitting on the curb were two brand new beach balls."

Praying for the Nations

During mission trips, we found that it was a great time to incorporate prayer for the nations of the 10/40 Window. We hung multiple posters up on the walls that each had a map and information about a country and the spiritual condition there. For example, Afghanistan is 90% Sunni Muslim, 9.7% Shia Muslim, and .3% other religion. Many times when children saw these countries and their spiritual condition, they became brokenhearted. Sandi St. Claire shared,

> I want to talk about last night. I know that my kids have been saved for a while. I know that they love the Lord, and they would do anything that He would ask them to do. Something happened last night. They realized that there are people dying and going to

hell, and it broke their hearts in a way I haven't seen in a while in Christians—adult Christians. I haven't seen it in anybody. It was more than just these people are dying and going to hell. It was, "What are we going to do about it?"

Brandi (adult leader) was on her first mission trip with preteens in 2018 in Cedar Hill, Texas. She was completely caught off guard by what she observed. Here is her perspective of what she witnessed:

This is our church's first mission trip. Last night, we were praying, and I was blown away. I have never seen kids pray for over an hour for other countries, other kids, and other kids in other countries. It was amazing. Then, you take something so powerful that happened last night and you compound that on to today. I am a children's minister, and this is the first time I have had children under my leadership lead someone to the Lord. I am overwhelmed and blown away by how God can use our kids. It's amazing to me.

Each child sees God's bigger picture in different ways—the desire that all people groups come to know their rightful King. Shelby (6th grade) was taken back by what she found out about the nation of Israel and its spiritual condition. Here is her story:

Hi, my name is Shelby, and so I just want to talk about what happened last night because it was the worst prayer walk and the best prayer walk I have ever had. So, if you know me, I don't cry a lot. Even my own cousin said that was the first time she's ever seen me cry. Because I was walking around, and I was already bawling. But, whenever I got to Israel...sorry (she starts to cry), that just broke my heart because Jesus walked on that Earth. He walked on our Earth. Israel is where He was born and where He walked and where He shared about God. And He shared that He was the Son of God, and that was where He was crucified. And only three percent of that population believes in Him. I was expecting to see 100% just because those are God's chosen people.

And I think that's why we're here. It's just, I think we were all meant to just go out into the world and just make those 3 percent...or 1 percent...just grow into 80 or even more because God deserves every single soul out there.

It is apparent that as children are put in situations that are out of their control or out of what is comfortable to them, they draw closer in their walk with Christ. Their prayer life deepens, and they turn to God for power and strength. Olivia (6th grade) shared, "This week, God has really put me and Him closer together. I have been praying a lot more to Him and reading the Bible more. He has shown me His power and that I can talk to Him a lot more."

Talk with God (Prayer and Personal Worship)

"Satan dreads nothing but prayer. His one concern is to keep the saints from praying. He fears nothing from prayerless studies, prayerless work, prayerless religion. He laughs at our toil, he mocks our wisdom, but he trembles when we pray." —Samuel Chadwick

Prayer intensifies amidst ministry with children and on mission trips. What that means is when children are ministering, they quickly become in tune with their Heavenly Father. Zachary shared,"We just stopped what we were doing and prayed for people to come...courage, strength, and not to lose hope. Then a few minutes later, a bunch of little kids came. It was amazing because we taught the story, and two people got saved. That's just amazing."

As the children minister, God speaks to them and answers their prayers. Kimberly (5th grade) shared, "I was doing the music, and I was trying to teach them the motions. I was still kind of nervous because it was my first time. I kind of felt really weird. Then I heard a voice in my head saying, 'Kimberly, seriously you can do it.' Then all of a sudden, I started being like myself and acting crazy. The kids started dancing right away and had a lot of fun."

When our preteens have talked to lost children and they were not ready to receive Christ, we witnessed the preteens catch a burden for their salvation. We watched them cry and sometimes weep for hours for specific lost children during our prayer times on these trips. They often get the opportunity to lead those children to Christ the next day or before the end of the week. If you want to ignite children's hearts in prayer, take them out into your community or on an evangelistic mission trip.

While counseling with children who respond to the Gospel, spiritual warfare is happening. Many times, the person being counseled appears to be blinded to the truth. When kids pray, the one they are counseling often opens their heart to the truth. Carri (5th grade) shared her experience, "Well, today I counseled this little girl named Matti. I knew that she was ready, so when I started counseling, I started praying for her. I don't really know what I said. I started praying and after I prayed, she told me that she wanted to accept Him into her heart."

The more we take them out of their comfort zones, the more we see God work in and through their lives. Worship becomes more powerful, ministry becomes more powerful, and we personally witness God's work in unique ways. It is easy to do ministry in the church, but it becomes more complicated when we take children out into the community. However, it is an eye-opening, life-changing experience for them.

Here are several things I have learned about teaching children to pray:

- Pray alongside them.
- Pray regularly.
- Pray before ministry.
- Pray before small group time.
- Pray on the armor of God. Pray it aloud and visualize putting on each piece.
- Pray before sharing the Gospel, for power from the Holy Spirit.
- Pray when a need arises.

- Pray when things get out of control.
- Pray and thank God when things go right.

Their Faith Is Developed by Observing Their Peers

One of our observations across multiple mission trips was leaders feeling bothered by the idea of not planning out the whole week. We have a set schedule, but we do not plan out the week for the ministry sites; we allow the Spirit to lead them daily. Allowing the Holy Spirit to move freely is a must. Leaders typically want to plan out who will share their testimony, who will teach the lesson, who will lead songs, who will lead games, who will counsel, etc. All these are parts of the weekly schedule on the mission trip.

However, we have learned to let the preteens and students pray and plan for the next day one day at a time. Adults step back and let them pray, and they learn together. They learn to listen to the Holy Spirit and His guidance. Often, the shyest preteens or students begin to listen to the Holy Spirit and feel compelled to teach or lead by the end of the week.

As they observe their peers, they gain confidence that they can do the same. They step out and trust God, and He uses them in powerful ways. By planning out and laying out the whole week, we eliminate the many times the Holy Spirit leads in a different way. We often times set up an immovable structure and just go through the motions apart from the power and leading of the Holy Spirit.

Breaking Down Spiritual Strongholds Through Prayer

Children are spiritual prayer warriors. In their innocence, they come before the throne of God and become a powerful force in ministry. The key is to have them pray and to pray with them intentionally. Have them pray for specific ministry needs in your church or community. Praying for God's presence and power in Kingdom work lights a fire in their hearts. During community outreach or mission trips, we often employ the following strategy when faced with challenging circumstances. These situations create excellent teaching times for children and students.

- Recognize the problem.
- Confess known sin in your life.
- Armor up!.
- Pray for God to intervene.
- Watch and see how God answers.
- Accept God's answer.
- When God moves, celebrate with a time of worship and praise.

On one mission trip, Cassady (6th grade) was at a government housing project with her father. She shared, "These birds flew up by where we were having our Bible study today. They kept going on and on, louder and louder. We went over by the tree they were in and prayed, and they stopped." Cassady's father later shared, "She walked over by the tree. When she bowed her head, the birds were immediately silenced, and we went on with our Bible study."

Pray with Children

Paul tells us to pray at all times (1 Thessalonians 5:17). We gave the children opportunity to pray regularly, and we prayed with them. Prayer is again something that is not taught but caught. If we wanted to develop prayer warriors, we recognized that our leaders needed to pray regularly with the children in our ministry.

We began by praying with the children in our church. We showed them how to pray and then listened to them while they prayed. Sometimes, in their innocence, they showed us how to pray. Children in the church can be trained up as an army of warriors for the King of kings that comes boldly to the throne of grace.

Our Wednesday evening director was walking down the hallway one day at our church. As he looked into a room through the window in the door, he saw one of our leaders, Mark, praying with the five boys that were in his group. He was modeling prayer for them and mentoring those boys how to pray. Mark was on his knees praying and so were all five 2nd-grade boys he was leading.

Teaching Children How to Pray

Prayer can be a natural flow from our hearts to our Heavenly Father. We know that we have direct access to the throne of grace any time, any day. Prayer acrostics can be effective tools for teaching children how to pray. These tools help them develop an attitude of worship, thanksgiving, repentance, and supplication.

P.R.A.Y. Acrostic (Isaiah 6:1-8)

Isaiah had an encounter with God that resulted in God calling him out in obedience to Him. Isaiah saw the angels worshipping God (vs. 1-4). He felt convicted of sin in the presence of God because of His holiness (v. 5), and Isaiah felt a burden for the people of Israel. Isaiah said, "I live among a people of unclean lips," (v. 5) and then he surrendered to God's will for his life: "Here am I. Send me!" (v. 8)

We discipled our preteens to bow before the Lord in prayer each day, praying in the Spirit as instructed in Ephesians 6:18. They were taught to approach the Lord humbly in worship and thanksgiving, to confess any known sin to Him, to ask the Lord what to pray for according to His will, and then to surrender themselves fully to His will for their lives every day.

- **P**raise and Thanksgiving (vs. 1–4)
- **R**epentance and Confession (v. 5)
- **A**sking (vs. 5b–7)
- **Y**ield and Surrender (v. 8)

As we went through the P.R.A.Y. acrostic, we found that there is a very similar effect on children across the board. When they praise God and worship Him, they experience His holy presence. This leads them to a time of confession in which the Holy Spirit reveals sin in their lives, just like He did with Isaiah.

After their time of confession and repentance, they begin to intercede for others. They pray in agreement with each other as they call out to the Lord. Finally, they make the ultimate holy sacrifice before God—surrender (Romans 12:1).

Children become more comfortable praying as they go through the prayer model again and again and develop it as a regular habit within their group. The goal of the P.R.A.Y. acrostic is to lead children to a life of daily surrender to Christ.

Prayer is the gateway to the Father. Through prayer, children can approach their Savior and then go out empowered by the Holy Spirit in ministry and in life. What a joy to teach children how to pray! Likewise, they can teach us. In their innocence, they can open the doors of Heaven and bring down the Kingdom of God on Earth.

No Longer a Slave to Fear

The following story comes from Alex and Diana Aburto, missionaries with Vine and Branches Ministries in Piedras Negras, Mexico. They have participated in multiple L.I.T. mission trips with us. They tell of how a young girl's life was changed as she learned to trust in the Lord and experience the power of the Holy Spirit working through her.

Valeria (former L.I.T.) has always been shy and introverted. She first came to know Jesus at a library ministry outreach when she was 7 years old. She told us plainly that she knew God wanted her to be a missionary. She began L.I.T. discipleship, wanting to grow in her faith to share Jesus with her parents. At library outreach, every day for 5 years, Valeria would ask for prayer for her parents to know Jesus. One day, she invited her parents to attend a ministry outreach, where her parents finally accepted Jesus.

As Valeria grew up, she struggled with expressing herself and often felt frustrated. When she turned 15, she accepted an invitation to co-mentor younger girls. The mentors were invited to join a local mission team for a week of community evangelism. She was hesitant about signing up for two reasons. She knew she would have to go door to door, meeting people, and her family was going through a crisis. Her grandmother had been very sick and in great pain for months. This crisis weighed heavy on her heart, and she struggled with expressing her concern.

When Valeria decided to trust God, she signed up to join the mission team. It was then when she became a witness to the powerful hand of God beginning to work, not only in her grandmother's health but in her own heart as well. The Lord greatly used Valeria that week to share the Gospel in the community. Valeria, a struggling introvert, suddenly recognized the power of the Holy Spirit.

One night with the mission team, she stood up before them to testify. She explained her struggles with fear and frustration in front of others. But she testified that each time she stepped out to share the Gospel with the mission team, she felt God responding by strengthening her in each word to the point that, without even knowing how, it became easy for her to talk with people. We witnessed how the power of God made a way for her fears to be left aside, and she was able to share the incredible gift of salvation with others. Weeks later, she testified that she continued to experience a strong conviction to share the Gospel.

A month later, Valeria and her brother were picking up their little sister from school when they recognized a lady from their week of missions and evangelism. The lady, a mother, explained she had now moved to their neighborhood. They felt God pushing them to *go further. Valeria realized this mother was passing through a crisis of her own. She prayed with her and wrote down her information. Valeria asked her own family to gather food, clothing, and toys, and that same day, they took them to the mother's house. She would never have had that encounter if she hadn't trusted God and signed up for the mission week. Valeria has experienced the power of the Holy Spirit and knows that God can use anyone if we only trust Him. Glory to God!*

Closing Prayer

I will close this chapter with a special prayer by a preteen while on a mission trip. At the end of our Hollister mission trip in 2015, McKayla (6th grade) prayed,

Dear Lord, I thank You that we had the opportunity to come here and impact the lives of everyone in this city. I pray that this city, that all the people here, will just learn more about You and grow in faith. And the seeds that have been planted in these children and adults this week, help them to be watered and harvested. Help them to share with others about what they have seen, too. In Jesus' name, Amen.

CHAPTER 9

Moving from Missions
Education to Missions

You have to ask yourself what is happening to the Christian church in America. Studies show that "80-85% of churches (in America) are plateaued or declining." [31] That is unbelievable. That is unacceptable. Where does the problem lie, and what can we do to change it? We have to return to the core of what the Church is about—the Great Commission. Somehow, so many of us have jumped ship; the train has come off the tracks.

We will never see the power of God in a stagnant church as long as we are not aligned with God's will. We will not see Him move in powerful ways apart from the Gospel of Jesus Christ—the Great Commission. That is why we exist—to "Go" and make disciples of the nations.

A recent study by Barna Research found that 51 percent of U.S. churchgoers had never heard of the Great Commission. [32] Twenty-five percent had heard of it but did not know what it is. Only about 17 percent understood what the Great Commission means. Sadly, this was the last command that Jesus gave His disciples before departing the earth. As the Church, we must turn to Christ's priorities and not man's priorities.[33]

In my church, we had a missions education program. I thought it was beautiful, all the stories of missionaries and what the Lord was doing through their lives. The kids would see their clothing and taste the food from many different countries. I found myself thinking, "Why are we only talking about missionaries? Why not become missionaries of the Gospel?"

During the summer of 2002, I did just that. I trained our preteens how to share their faith and then released them to do so. Wow! My eyes were opened, and I realized that this was a missing piece to the puzzle. We would truly see preteens we were discipling "get it" when they led someone to Christ for the first time. One leader shared, "It was like a match that lit a fire."

Everyone Is Called to Go

It is funny how many people think of every excuse in the world not to share their faith. The top reason people do not share their faith is fear. The second is they do not know how; they have never been taught. I can understand fear. I have had those times myself. But the second is our problem. If people do not know how to share their faith, that falls back on the Church. My gift is evangelism, and according to Ephesians 4:11-13, I am called to equip the saints for works of ministry. "And He Himself gave some to be apostles, some prophets, some evangelists, and some pastors and teachers, for the equipping of the saints for the work of ministry." So, I put my gift to use. I worked together with other evangelists in my church and other organizations and came up with a tool to train children.

Proper Training Is a Must

Proper training is a must. We should never take sharing the Gospel lightly, but it is not so complicated that we have to have a seminary education to share. For some reason, pastors and leaders are afraid to equip their people to share the Gospel. There is no excuse for this we are all called to share God's redemptive story of salvation through the death, burial, and resurrection of Christ. That story is simple enough for a child to lead their family to the Savior.

When we started training children to counsel lost people, we taught them discernment. Like us, if they are believers, they have the Holy Spirit dwelling in them. They understand that we are not doing this for numbers; we are doing it for God's glory. We give them a tool that has all open-ended questions that help them discern where a child or person is spiritually. They know that if a person does not understand they have sinned or know what sin is, they are probably not ready.

If they are not a sinner, then they are not in need of a Savior. Jesus tells us, "And when He has come, He will convict the world of sin, and of righteousness, and of judgment of sin, because they do not believe in Me" (John 16:8-9). For preteens on mission, we have witnessed them truly heartbroken over lost children. When they counsel a child who does not comprehend what sin is or believe that they have ever sinned, it is really upsetting to our preteens.

We have had seen them testify before the group, "I talked with a little boy today. He just did not understand what sin is. Please pray that he will understand that He has sinned and that he needs Jesus. Some kids are even more aggressive in their statements: "I am going to pray that they understand that they have sinned so I can lead them to Christ tomorrow." "We are going to get these kids to understand that they have sinned and they need Jesus."

One of the adult leaders who attended our Tulsa, Oklahoma, trip shared, "I saw kids pray and weep for hours for kids they met at the site for their salvation." As the Holy Spirit works in children, they become even more sensitive to the lost condition of children. They can discern whether they are ready or not to make a decision for Christ. Many times, they will pray for a child and then end up leading them to Christ the next day.

If You Train Them, They Will GO

As we began to train children in our church, they became fearless in sharing their faith. I had one preteen approach me one day and ask me for a Bible for her friend. She said, "I led her to Christ at school." Before long, she asked me again and again for Bibles and new Christian materials. I asked her one day, "How many people have you led to Christ?" She asked, "This year or last year?" I said, "This year," and she said, "Five."

I made it a goal to train everyone in my ministry on how to share their faith. With children, they do not know better than to share the Gospel with everyone they know. I am saying this sarcastically. They are fearless once you train them. One father came to me and said, "Clint, I need for you to talk with Brooklyn. She is telling everyone about Christ at school. I am afraid she is going to get kicked out of school. She catches kids on the playground, pulls them to the side, and asks them if they know Christ. Then she tells them about Him if they are not believers."

Training Kids Outside the Church

My heart has always been to reach children in my church and outside my church with the Gospel. It is my passion that they might know the Savior. While I served in Fort Worth, we were blessed with the opportunity to do afterschool Bible clubs in 11 public schools. We prayed intently for open doors to get into certain schools. We had prayed for more than three years to get into a school called Greenbriar Elementary.

One day the principal called and said, "You have my permission to start the afterschool Bible club. Shortly afterward, I had the opportunity to teach the lesson. As I drove to the school, I was thinking, "Lord, I have told the story of Zacchaeus probably a hundred times." I was almost frustrated at the idea of teaching this story again.

There were about 30 children that day. As I stood up and started teaching the story, I came to the part where Zacchaeus was in the tree and Jesus walked up to him. Jesus said, "Zacchaeus, come down from there, for salvation has come to your household today." Right then, it hit me that we had been praying for this school for more than three years, and salvation had come to them today.

I said, "Boys and girls, we have been praying for over three years to get into your school so that we could tell you about Jesus and His love for you." Just like Zacchaeus, salvation has come to you today." From there, I invited them to respond to the Gospel message. I said, "If you would like to trust Christ as your Savior and Lord, please raise your hand."

Everyone in the room raised their hand. I thought to myself that they must have misunderstood.

Then I explained the Gospel to them again and said, "If you would like to trust Christ, please go into the hallway so that we can talk with you." They all moved into the hallway to be counseled. For the next several weeks, we talked to them about making a decision. The majority of the children had truly made a decision for Christ.

Shortly afterward, we began teaching them how to walk with Christ daily. We also taught all of them how to share their faith. We took them step-by-step through the message and how to lead someone to Christ. The following week, we asked them if they had told anyone about Christ last week? Most of them raised their hands.

Then we asked more specifically if any of them had led someone to Christ in the past week. The majority raised their hands again. Some had led brothers and sisters, cousins, and friends to Christ. One little boy said, "I led my mom and dad to Christ." Right then, I wanted to follow up with this family. A few days later, I went to pay a visit with the family. I knocked on the door and the little boy's mother answered. We talked for a bit and then I asked her, "I heard that you accepted Christ as your Savior and Lord." She said, "Yes, he led me to Christ." She pointed to her son. Her little boy was in 3rd grade—nine years old. He was only nine years old, and he led his mom to Christ. I am still amazed by this.

Taking the Gospel into the Schools

My goal was to get our preteens off-campus from our church to give them an opportunity to minister and share the Gospel. We hosted events in 11 public schools. We trained them at the church, and when we got to the school, we announced to the children at the event that it was going to be led by kids. Watching our preteens lead out in front of approximately 400 children was amazing to watch. They shined His glory.

Many times, my leadership would question my judgment. They did not feel like our preteens were ready, but when it came time, they stepped up and the Lord used them in powerful ways. On one occasion, I asked a 5th-grade boy named Mark to share the Gospel at the conclusion of the event. He stepped up on stage and shared the Wordless Book. When he came to the invitation, he asked the kids in the audience to raise their hands if they wanted to accept Christ. Hands popped up all over the auditorium that evening. There were 40 children who accepted Christ.

On one occasion, we hosted the event at a school that was more than 80 percent Hispanic. We went through our full event that evening. There were children as well as parents in attendance that evening. We decided to have the Gospel message translated from English to Spanish. Haley (6th grade) got up on stage and an older gentleman who was a former missionary followed. She would say a sentence, and he would translate it into Spanish. Haley shared, and the gentleman translated throughout her whole message. At the end, she gave an invitation to respond to the Gospel, and many people got up and walked into our counseling room. There were at least 40 people who accepted Christ that evening. They came to know Him through a 6th grader.

Confidence in Sharing my Faith by Zoe Brown (former L.I.T.; 18 years old)

I started L.I.T. when I was in 4th grade, and it shaped me into the person I am today. When I became "too old" to participate in L.I.T., I started to disciple two young girls, and I was able to watch them grow in their faith. L.I.T. showed me not only the importance of a daily walk with Christ but also the importance of discipleship. If it wasn't for L.I.T., I probably would not have gone on overseas missions like I have the past three years. L.I.T. gave me confidence when it came to sharing my faith with others.

Vacation Bible School Run by Kids

As I observed children sharing the Gospel, I realized that I must become intentional in training them to be missionaries. It became apparent that the easiest place to do so was in the community right around our church. There were limitations put on them in our church because of the way we programmed events, so one year I decided to take our Vacation Bible School into three public schools.

When we did VBS in the church, there were limited places where our preteens and students could serve. We had an adult or a few adult leaders who pretty much did everything. We had music, recreation, crafts, snacks, and Bible study, and a few adults pretty much did everything. It was an adult run VBS, and our kids were spectators in the event.

So, we took VBS offsite, and the majority of our church loved it. Our kids helped lead worship, they taught or helped with crafts, helped or taught recreation, and served snacks. It was beautiful watching the body of Christ in full function outside the church building. The number of decisions that were made that year nearly tripled.

The following year, we took VBS into local apartment complexes. Again, our preteens and students shined. They took on leadership roles and ministered to children and their families. One parent of some children that attended said, "I have never seen a church do this before. It is amazing that you have come to where we live." It was a joy as we mobilized our kids into the community.

When we adopted this format of ministry, it opened doors for our preteens and students. Otherwise, they would not have had a place to serve and minister using their spiritual gifts. By doing this, they flourished in their gifts.

One of my greatest joys every year is our preteen mission trip. "When the adults got out of the way, the Holy Spirit did a work," one adult leader stated. Through the years as I have trained leaders and prepared for the mission trip, it has been such a joy to watch the transformation happen in the lives of children, preteens, and students. It does not take long to realize that this is God's plan because He shows up in the midst of making His name famous.

We have learned that a month before our mission trip, we intentionally train them. These are typical elements of our training.

1. Developing each one's personal testimony to share on the trip
2. Daily quiet times to prepare for teaching the lesson
3. Role-playing and being prepared to counsel the lost
4. Practicing the evangelistic Bible study
5. Learning mission trip songs and motions
6. Praying and preparing their hearts before the trip

By intentionally training preteens, they arrive at the mission location ready to go. Oh, they are terrified many times. You can see it in their eyes when they arrive from various churches. Some almost become ill in fear of teaching, leading worship, or sharing their testimony. The amazing thing is that fear turns into God's supernatural power.

Jim Cymbala shares, "I discovered an astonishing truth: God is attracted to weakness. He can't resist those who humbly and honestly admit how desperately they need Him." [34] This so true in preteens, or anyone else, in the midst of ministry and missions. They are fearful, they cry out to Him, and He takes over with power. Many preteens are never the same after experiencing the power of the Holy Spirit in their lives on these trips.

It is such a joy watching them trying to explain what they have experienced. As I shared earlier, this is the typical testimony that we have heard so many times: "God spoke through me today. But I don't remember a word I said" or "The Holy Spirit poured over me today." The Holy Spirit shows up so powerful when we are obedient to fulfill the Great Commission.

Some Leaders Just Don't Get It

On one of our mission trips in Fort Worth, we had churches from five states come together for this trip. We combined churches into small groups of ten. Sometimes, a group was made up of people from two churches. As the week progressed, many of them would become lifelong friends. One day on this trip, a leader came to me particularly upset. She said, "Karen took over at the site today. She did everything and did not let the kids lift a finger."

The two leaders and I sat down together to discuss the problem. Karen said, "I am an evangelist at heart. When we got there, I felt led to call all the children together and share the Gospel with them. It was great—the majority of them accepted Christ." I said, "Karen, I understand your gift of evangelism, but wouldn't it have been even more amazing to allow the preteens in your group to lead out? You robbed them of an opportunity to lead someone to Christ and experience the joy of this wonderful privilege." Our goal is to step back, let them be missionaries, and allow them to do everything.

On our first mission trip to Corpus Christi, I had a public schoolteacher named Rachel who went on the trip with us. At the time, I was not aware that she was not sure about our preteens teaching and ministering to children. I made it a habit to drive from ministry site to ministry site on mission trips. I loved to pop in and encourage the preteens and leaders as they served. Well, as I walked in the door at one site, I found Rachel (the adult) standing in front of the children teaching the lesson. I gently pulled her aside and said, "Rachel, remember this is their mission trip."

While in Catoosa, Oklahoma, one year, we had a church travel as far as North Carolina to be on the mission trip with us. It took them almost two full days to get there. They were so excited to be able to join us. Their kids were prepared and fired up to go out and share the Good News of Christ. Around the third day, one of the leaders from the North Carolina church came to me sincerely upset. She said, "We have worked so hard to prepare our group to have an opportunity to counsel with a lost child. Today when the invitation was given, a little girl raised her hand, and the student pastor from _____ church took the little girl aside and led her to Christ. Our kids are so disappointed." I had to remind the student pastor that this was the kids' mission trip. It is our intention to allow them to share, and we step back and watch and observe.

It is extremely difficult at times for some adults to release children as missionaries. They just do not get how important it is for our children to be successful in the body of Christ...to allow them to be missionaries... to allow the mentee to become the mentor...to release this generation to fulfill their part of the Great Commission.

Kids Counseling at Camp

I cannot count the number of times that children's pastors and preteen leaders have called me saying, "You won't believe what happened at camp last week!" A lot of churches returned home from the mission trip and immediately packed up and headed to camp.

During the worship times at camp, the leader would give an invitation for kids to receive Christ. To their surprise, a number of kids that had gone on the mission trip would grab their Bibles and head down the aisle to counsel the lost children who came forward. Adults from other churches often did not feel comfortable counseling, and they would stay in their seats. The camp leaders were amazed that preteens knew how to counsel and would be so bold as to come to the front to do so.

If You Go, He Will Show Up

As I shared earlier, one of my gifts is evangelism...mostly child evangelism. I have seen thousands of children come to know Christ in the past 33 years of ministry, the majority of which were led to Christ by children and preteens. In all my years of ministry, the Holy Spirit shows up more powerfully on mission for Christ.

I have attended camps, revivals, retreats, crusades, and so much more, but I have never seen the presence of God more powerful than when we are about sharing His redemptive story. That tells me that the Gospel is a priority to God. This is confirmed from what we read in His Word but also by the presence and power of the Holy Spirit showing up and working in the lives of children, preteens, and students (Acts 1:8).

We never know how the Holy Spirit might show up, but He does, in the middle of a Gospel presentation or when children testify of their salvation. It is unexplainable how He uses kids to share His amazing message, but He does. This is what we are about so that every tribe, nation, and tongue will stand before the throne and the Lamb (Revelation 7:9).

Kids Can Reach Kids "Easierly"

One of my favorite things to do is to interview kids and leaders on mission trips. Their stories are a joy to hear. On our mission trip to Granbury in 2015, I interviewed a little girl named Emma Grace. Emma was in 4th grade at the time.

> So, when we went to the Boys and Girls Club today, we had 25 kids. We had a great time. There was this one boy that when I did the Bible study today....When I was doing the Bible study, some of the kids weren't paying attention, but he paid attention really well. So, I asked, "If anyone would like to accept Christ today, please raise your hand." So, he raised his hand, and I got partnered up with him and sat in the hallway. He really knew that Jesus died on the cross for us and that God loved all of us.

I asked Emma, "Did he understand what sin is?"

Emma: "Yes."

Me: "Do you feel confident that he came to know the Lord today?"

Emma: "Yes."

Me: "Did you know that there were three other kids who came to know

Christ?"

Emma: "Yes."

Me: "You're a kid and you are teaching. How did you do that?"

Emma: "What do you mean?"

Me: "I just thought kids couldn't do this kind of stuff. What is your opinion on that?"

Emma: "In my perspective, I really think when grownups talk to kids, they get a little more shy, because it's like, an adult. But when it's a kid talking with a kid, it's like a best friend. You really have your best friend there. You can talk with her about anything, and you can't always do that with adults sometimes. But when you're talking with a kid, it's more comfortable, where you can talk to them easierly."

What It Means to Step Up and Be a Leader by *Jadyn Elkins Toliver (L.I.T. 2011-2012)*

From the teachings of L.I.T., I have learned what it means to step up and be a leader. This gained character trait has not only aided me in the mission field but also in my relationships with the people around me. L.I.T. taught me the importance of having a daily quiet time, or time spent reading and listening to God's Word.

L.I.T. helped me fully understand the seriousness of sharing my faith with others and that the mission field does not disappear once we go home. Even as a young adult, these foundations are still a part of who I am, and I continue to use the tools that L.I.T. equipped me with to this day.

By the time Jadyn was 18 years old, she had participated in 14 mission trips, eight of which were international.

CHAPTER 10

Spiritual Gifts

"For as we have many members in one body, but all the members do not have the same function, so we, being many, are one body in Christ, and individually members of one another. Having then gifts differing according to the grace that is given to us, let us use them: if prophecy, let us prophecy in proportion to our faith; or ministry, let us use it in our ministering; he who teaches, in teaching; he who exhorts, in exhortation; he who gives, with liberality; he who leads, with diligence; he who shows mercy, with cheerfulness." (Romans 12:4-8)

I believe one of the biggest surprises to me was discovering that children have spiritual gifts from the Holy Spirit. For so long, everything I read applied to me and other adults and maybe some youth, but certainly not to children. But, when I got out of the way and quit hindering God from working in the lives of children, their gifts were evident right before my eyes. It is so tempting to set kids aside to be seen and not heard. I believe that is the problem in the Church today.

You see, no one likes to sit on the bench in sports and watch everyone else play. No—they want to be IN the game! God is calling them off the bench and letting them join Him in His story. Friends, we are not finished as the Church until every tribe, nation, and tongue stand before the throne and the Lamb in worship (Revelation 7:9). God has gifted every believing child with the ability to join the Church and fulfill the mission.

The gifts exist there in your church, but children are being sidelined. One day, a 9-year-old girl named Carilyn approached me at my church and asked, "Is there anything you need done?" I took her down the hallway to our resource room and let her have at it. About an hour later, she knocked on my door and said, "I'm finished. Is there anything else you need me to do?" We walked down the hallway to the resource room, and it was perfect. She had put everything in ideal order. I thought later, "She has the gift of administration and organization."

As I began to recognize these gifts, it became an exciting challenge for me to find creative ways to help more children in my church discover their gifts. I find that there is no greater joy in ministry than to use my spiritual gifts to serve and build up the body of Christ. I wanted the same for the children in my church. I figured that the only way this could be accomplished was through our small groups. So, I encouraged our teachers and small group leaders to allow children to serve alongside them in their groups.

One of our leaders started encouraging the boys in his group to teach on a regular basis. From that group, we discovered two young men who had the gift of teaching. I began to stretch them and give them opportunities to use their gifts before larger groups and sometimes before large crowds. Through this, they learned to allow the Holy Spirit to minister through them. I found some children who were natural leaders. They could go in front of large groups of children and take the lead. The younger children would practically eat out of their hands.

GIFTS AND MINISTRY

Spiritual gifts provide every believer, including children and students, with spiritual purpose and identity in the Church. One of the paradigms we must break is the 80/20 rule. [35] For many churches, only 20 percent of the people do the ministry while the remaining 80 percent are recipients. This model limits the number of places where children and students can serve.

Frequently, leaders consider children only to be seen and not heard, which compounds the problem. Not to mention the issue that numerous adults do not realize children have spiritual gifts themselves. But even if adults accept the fact that children have gifts, they hold that children are not mature enough to serve or minister. Can they serve in the body of

Christ? Ogden writes, "Every member of the body comes to know his or her value through the exercise of spiritual gifts. To the extent that members of the body are not playing their part, the whole body suffers." [36]

Children Have Spiritual Gifts That Are Relevant for Ministry Today

What I hope to do in this chapter is to give you a bigger picture. There is a multitude of gifts in the body of Christ, and as Paul said in Romans 12:4-8, they all have a role in the body of Christ. The pastor could not preach on a Sunday morning without all the other gifts in the church in full function. He needs all the gifts working together to grow the local church—the body of Christ. Let us explore the amazing gifts of children.

Organization/Administration (1 Corinthians 12:28)

Titus was to organize the ministry in Crete. The person with the organization/administration gift helps the Church organize itself so it can effectively minister to its own members and to others out in the world. I have observed in my church and on multiple mission trips children and students alike with this gift. They will take the lead in organizing the group for ministry. They enjoy such tasks as keeping records and performing administrative duties.

For the past 16 years, I have been on numerous mission trips with preteens and students. I have learned through the years to take advantage of preteens and students who want to serve using their gifts. When Hannah was in 8th grade, she started helping with meals on our mission trip. She learned how to prepare meals for hundreds of preteens and leaders on these mission trips. She was also in charge of making sure every ministry site had enough food to feed the children that were there.

On one of our mission trips, the kitchen director was unable to go on the trip. We considered Hannah and determined that she could handle the job. Hannah was 18 years old at the time. She, along with four other teenagers, prepared 1,700 plates in seven days with minimal adult supervision. They fed some 180 preteens and leaders on the trip as well as all the children from the community who attended our sites.

Giving

The gift of giving expresses itself in a desire to give above and beyond our ten percent tithe. The person with this gift finds it easy to give freely and has a cheerful attitude in doing so. While we were on our mission trip in Norman, we ministered at a local apartment complex. We saw about 30 eviction notices posted on doors throughout the complex. It was sad that so many families were desperate to keep a roof over their heads. Grace was overwhelmed with the needs of these people. She asked a mother of some children they were ministering to if there was anything she needed. The lady told her, "We don't have any food in our home for our kids." Grace was deeply heartbroken for the family, so she went before our entire group that evening and shared her deep concern for this family's need. We asked the kids on the mission trip if they would like to give to help this family. The next morning, we took up an offering and collected more than $275 to give to this family.

Grace saw the need, and she and the people on the mission trip gave to meet this family's needs. They purchased a gift card and took it to the mother. When the mother saw the card, she broke down in tears of joy. She rejoiced at what God had done for her family through a bunch of kids. Grace saw a need, and she found a way to meet that need with the help of many others.

At another site during our Sapulpa mission trip, there were children arriving at the Bible study wearing their older siblings' shoes. There were five children all wearing oversized shoes, including toddlers in teen-size sandals. That week, the preteens in the group took their spending money that they had brought on the trip and purchased three pairs of shoes for each child. When they delivered the shoes to the family, the mother just broke down crying at the doorway of their home.

Service

The gift of service is evident when a person genuinely desires to serve others. They find it easy to be a servant in the church and experience great joy and fulfillment in doing so. It is apparent that kids love to serve in the church. They are always looking for ways to help. But there is a specific gift of service that certain individuals in the body of Christ have. I learned that there were certain preteens and students who would do just about anything for me. There was never a question; they would just take off and do whatever I asked with a joyful attitude.

When we arrived for our mission trip in Hollister, the host church bathrooms needed to be cleaned. Before I said a word, here came Shane with a mop, bucket, and all the cleaning supplies. He went through all the bathrooms and made sure they were clean all week long. The funny thing is, I never asked him to do it! He found genuine pleasure in serving and just did it.

Micah was one of our up-and-coming servant-leaders. I could ask him to clear a room, and he would grab his music player, put his earbuds in, and have at it. It would be set up perfectly just like I asked him. One day, I asked him to share the responsibilities with some of the preteens on the mission trip. He struggled at first, but he modeled for them what it meant to be a servant.

Evangelism

The gift of evangelism is the ability to explain clearly to lost people how to become Christians and to persuade them to desire to be saved. Many of the children in our churches today possess the gift of evangelism. I have seen this gift in children combined with the gift of shepherd. Following many of our mission trips, preteens return home with a passion to continue their mission. Their gift of evangelism is present, and they freely share their faith with kids in their own neighborhoods and schools.

Matti returned home and thought about her friends at school who did not know Christ. She talked to her mom about starting a Bible study at her school, and weeks later, she started. She shared, "I have led four of the girls in my Bible study to the Lord. I am praying that the other three will receive the Lord as well."

Sarah went home from a mission trip in San Marcos and felt compelled to reach the children in her neighborhood. We provided her with the supplies she needed to host a Bible club at a park in her neighborhood. There were four children attending, and by the end of the week, she had led all four of them to Christ.

Prophecy

The gift of prophecy enables a person to speak God's Word boldly so that it brings conviction of sin. Prophets speak to people and confront them concerning sin. The gift of prophecy is a powerful gift. I watched a young man (Trent) in Jersey Village near Houston stand before approximately 150 children and adults and proclaim the Gospel. God spoke through him so powerfully as he quoted one passage of Scripture after another. He gave an invitation, and some 30 or so people received Christ as Savior.

About a month later, Trent and another young lady from my church traveled to South America with their fathers, who were leading the trip. Trent's father Jeff shared what happened on their trip:

> We traveled up the Amazon River to reach the Yagua people. When we would arrive at a village, we would invite the villagers to the center of the town to share Christ. When the adults shared, the people really didn't slow down. But when Trent and Katherine stood up and taught, everything was perfectly quiet. There wasn't even a baby crying. The Yagua people thought that if a child spoke, it must have been a message from God.

Avery was a preteen with the gift of prophecy. She had a different way about her. Some prophets have difficulty with the issue of grace; Avery was known to "say it like it is." There were no gray areas; it was always black and white. She tended to confront sin with little grace or mercy. She obviously had the gift of prophecy; however, she needed to learn to show grace.

When Jordan spoke during our testimony time, it was like hearing a prophet share. He was 11 years of age at the time, but he spoke with such boldness that you just knew it came from the Holy Spirit. His message was so powerful that when we shared the video of it later at our church, it deeply impacted many who heard it. Jordan's message still affects a lot of people when they hear it during our training events.

Teaching

The gift of teaching is the ability to convey Bible truths in a way that others might understand and be built up in their faith. I often mention the gift of teaching because it really amazes me that a child can stand up in front of a group of children their age or younger and teach with such eloquence. I have ministered in afterschool Bible clubs for the past 14 years. As I began to discover that children had gifts, I intentionally gave them opportunities to teach and lead.

I served in a school in Aledo, Texas, two years ago, helping with an afterschool Bible study. I was working with the 5th graders at the time. There was a little girl in my group named Claire who had somewhat of a speech impediment. During my time there, we started allowing the 5th graders to teach the younger children from kindergarten up.

One day, I was in a group with Claire. She was given the opportunity to teach a kindergarten group. She just stood up and took the lead and taught those kids as if she had been doing it all her life. I was truly amazed at what a gifted teacher she was. The kids were mesmerized and believed her teaching without question. She was patient and very loving to them. It was such a blessing to watch.

Bryan started teaching a group of children in a small group when he was in 6th grade. His disciple group leader had Bryan serving alongside him teaching kindergarten at his church. Through these consistent opportunities, Bryan developed his gift of teaching. He became a confident teacher because of regular opportunities to serve.

Grace told her dad that she felt called to teach when she was in 5th grade. Her dad said "sure," and she began her journey as a teacher. The amazing thing is that her assistant in the classroom was an adult who learned to step back and allow Grace to thrive in her gifts.

Elizabeth began teaching 2nd graders when she was in 5th grade. She went to her own Sunday school class during the first hour of church and then helped teach a group of 2nd graders during the second hour. Amazingly, Elizabeth taught all the way through her 12th grade year. She, like many children, has the gift of teaching. God can and will use children when they are given the opportunity to teach.

Encouragement/Exhortation

Romans 12:6-8 lists several gifts of the Spirit, including the gift of encouragement, or exhortation. It is given to build up the body of Christ. The person with the gift of encouragement easily edifies other people, helps build confidence, and reminds Christians of the hope they have in Christ.

If you watch children, there are many who have the gift of encouragement. Breanne started working with us on our mission trips when she was in 5th grade. She regularly served on the mission trips, taking on administrative and leadership roles. I observed her on many occasions speaking words to build up children and students on the trip. She was such a joy to see in full operation.

Micah Galey (former L.I.T.) was one who could step up in front of a group of kids and teach, and they walked away encouraged by what they heard from him. He had the God-given gift of encouragement. When he taught, even as a teenager, the kids loved him deeply. He never used harsh words in his teaching. The preteens and leaders were constantly edified and built up after hearing or spending time with Micah.

Shepherd/Leadership

The shepherd, or pastor, is gifted by the Holy Spirit to be a leader. He has the ability and desire to teach, protect, and build up the church.

Pastor Joel Hayworth began serving in the church when he was in 5th grade. He taught on a regular basis and served in the worship band as well. Throughout his varied experiences in the church, he gained confidence as a teacher and mentor. His passion grew, and he began a Bible study at his church for students. He shared, "One of the things that has shaped me is using my spiritual gifts in the local church. Because of L.I.T., though, I learned that God had given me a gift, and I have a responsibility to use that gift to further the kingdom of God."

When Holland was 12 years old, he taught the children's sermon in front of our church. He was speaking in front of close to 900 people that day, and he did an amazing job! When he moved into junior high school, his family moved out of the area and began attending a different church. The youth pastor there saw such potential in Holland that he gave him a teaching position in the junior high class. Today, Holland is attending seminary and is training to be a minister. Holland shared, "That same sense of fulfillment that I first tasted in L.I.T.—of working toward an eternal purpose—is why I'm currently in seminary today and eager to pursue full-time ministry."

Out of concern for her friends at school, Matti started a Bible study with them. She knew her friends did not know Christ, so she got permission to start a weekly Bible club on campus. The beauty of what Matti did was, she became like a shepherd to her friends. She taught them the Word of God out of a desire for them to be saved and grow in their faith, just like she had done.

Mercy

Those who have the gift of mercy are intuitively aware of the needs of others and feel strongly compelled to help them. They are compassionate toward people around them who are in need.

Valeria (15 years old) went through some terribly difficult times in her life. When she met a lady and realized this mother was facing a crisis of her own, Valeria prayed with her and wrote down her contact information.

Valeria asked her own family to gather food, clothing, and toys, and that same day, they took the items to the mother's house. Valeria experienced the power of the Holy Spirit and now knows that God can use anyone if we only trust Him. Glory to God! [37]

The gift of mercy particularly expresses itself through children when they are taken to some rough places on mission. We have been in government housing projects, drug-infested mobile home parks, and apartment complexes in low-income neighborhoods in multiple cities. Christian children with the gift of mercy become impassioned to help children in these situations, either by feeding them or taking on their burdens in a personal way. They are willing to give up their own lunches so that children at some of these locations can have a meal.

We have had families in our church who regularly expressed this passion and helped with local food kitchens or with the food pantry in our church. This gift flows through them to meet the needs of those who are struggling in some way.

Faith

The gift of faith is an unwavering trust in what God promises. The person with the gift of faith believes that God will be faithful to His Word. We witnessed the gift of faith express itself through the prayers of preteens and students. Many of us have been truly amazed at how they can cry out to God one moment and then see God answer their prayers the next.

I believe we have seen many people come to know Christ because of kids praying for them. We saw a bold confidence in Kerrville, Texas, one summer. The kids went out and would meet children and share the Gospel with them. Many times, the child did not understand. It was not uncommon for children to be fervently determined as they testified in the evenings: "We are going to get this person for Christ. We are going to pray for them, and they are going to accept Jesus as their Savior."

Greg Taylor (leader) shared, "I have never seen kids like this saying, 'We are going to get this kid' or 'We are going to get these kids.' That just blows me away." This is not unusual when children learn how to pray. They pray for God's will, and God answers their prayers. It has been as simple as them praying for beach balls for a game and then driving up and finding the balls sitting on the curb at the park where they have planned to minister. Many children have the gift of faith, and they are powerful prayer warriors.

Children believe that God is going to move, and He does. They hear His Word and believe what it says. In amazement, we adults step back and glorify the Lord because of His heart for kids. If God says it—they believe it!

Helps

Christians with the gift of helps are those who like to work to assist or help another person's ministry. They usually work behind the scenes. Children with the gift of helps are usually those who want to serve behind the scenes. They do not want to be in front of a group of people.

Zane would come to his children's pastor every Sunday and ask how he could help. It might be setting up or going to get supplies. Helping and supporting the ministry was one of Zane's spiritual gifts, and he loved to serve.

While visiting a church near Houston, I was asked to sit in on a 6th grade Sunday school class. The teacher was a good friend, and he was excited for me to join them. I sat back and watched and really enjoyed hearing the preteens engaging in the lesson that day. As Marc closed the class in prayer and as the kids were leaving, I noticed one of the boys stuck around. He began to put all the chairs back into place. I asked Marc if this was something he had assigned the boy to do, and he replied, "No, he just does it every Sunday."

One of my biggest headaches in ministry has been working with media. I found myself stressed a lot of times trying to get ready on a Sunday morning or Wednesday evening. What I really needed was for someone else to run the sound system as well as our video projection system. Then, we started training our preteens how to run all our equipment. I got to where I could ask them to play certain songs, and they would get it all set up, including the words to the songs using ProPresenter. I loved it, and they loved it. When we would start our worship time, they ran the system from the back.

Other Gifts

There are multiple gifts I have not mentioned, and there are many diverse and different ministries in the Church today, including children, students, worship ministry, and others. The gifts listed above are from personal observance in children. The Holy Spirit is the One who bestows the gifts. It should be our goal to make sure every member of our church expresses their God-given gift(s). I have noticed that many children will typically first show that they have one gift. Then, as they grown in their faith, other gifts begin to manifest. One young lady in our church said that when she first took the spiritual gift test, she scored high in administration. When she took it again years later, it showed that she had multiple gifts.

What always blesses me is when a child discovers their gift, and they do not realize they even have a gift. Micah Galey (former L.I.T.) shared, "People said they thought I had the gift of teaching. As I have taught over the years, I realized maybe God has called me to teach." When they serve, it brings them pure joy to use their gifts to minister and bless others. Incredibly, they find their gifts while in the midst of doing ministry.

Unrealized Potential

While speaking several years ago on this topic of children serving, a children's pastor came up to me and said, "Clint, this is exactly what my children's pastor did for me and eleven other girls. She gave us opportunities to serve, teach lessons, and participate in other church ministry projects. All twelve of us are now in full-time ministry."

Can you imagine a day in which there are no leadership voids in the church? The lack of leadership can be so frustrating and problematic at times. The dilemma is that we have not trained ALL the leaders in the church to serve and build up the body of Christ. If you think about it, in most churches, 80 percent of the spiritual gifts are not being used—they are often sidelined. Children make up a large percentage of the spiritual gifts in the Church today.

Church became exciting for me when I was allowed to express myself through my spiritual gifts. The same is true for children. As you begin to take this journey, there will be resistance at first. But after a while, you will create a new normal in your church. People will start to see children as younger brothers and sisters in Christ and will do everything in their power to come alongside them to train them, equip them, and release them in ministry.

Sarah (6th grade) became the lead teacher of a 1st grade class during the second hour. Her assistant was a seminary student. The first Sunday she taught, a man brought his granddaughter to her class. Sarah greeted her at the door. The grandfather asked who the teacher was, and Sarah looked up and said, "Here I am!" The grandfather was a little surprised. Sarah's mom said that Sarah would spend almost four hours every Saturday preparing to teach her class. She would bake cookies and make her class special every week. She would show up early on Sunday mornings to lay out her classroom and have it ready for the kids when they came in.

L.I.T. Played a Significant Role in My Spiritual Life by Pastor Joel Hayworth (L.I.T. 2008-2009)

Joel Hayworth is Senior Pastor at Morgan Baptist Church in Conway, Arkansas.

Two things specifically that are a part of L.I.T. that have played significant roles in my spiritual formation are forming spiritual disciplines and using *spiritual gifts in the local church. As a young believer, I was given a weekly Scripture verse to memorize and a daily passage to read.*

These things might seem minor or even insignificant to some people, but to a young Christian, this was precisely what I needed to grow in my faith and knowledge of God's Word! A second thing that L.I.T. encouraged and has shaped me is using my spiritual gifts in the local church. Because of L.I.T., though, I learned that God had given me a gift, and I have a responsibility to use that gift to further the kingdom of God.

CHAPTER 11

What Do Kids Bring to the Table?

My greatest joy in the past 33 years has been growing together with these younger brothers and sisters in Christ—kids. They have taught me so much through their giftedness and abilities at such a young age. They have amazed me with their wisdom and insight. It sounds crazy, but if you allow them a voice, they, like young Samuel, will become a voice for Christ.

In Samuel's day, there were few new words from God. In some ways, our day is somewhat the same. "Now the boy Samuel was ministering to the Lord before Eli. And word from the Lord was rare in those days, visions were infrequent" (1 Samuel 3:1). Eli realized that God was speaking to Samuel, so he showed Samuel how to receive God's message. Should we not be doing the same for kids today?

God is speaking to the kids in our churches and communities, but are we listening to what He is saying? He is speaking and showing us that His plans and purposes include the children in our churches. God has given them a voice and a purpose to fulfill. When properly trained, they can become a powerful voice for the Great Commission.

Children will teach you about worship. During their worship, I have sat back and felt God's presence fall in the building. Their worship is pure and innocent. They do not have the distractions of life, like most adults, nor the baggage some of us might carry.

They have taught me that they do not have a baby Holy Spirit. The first time I heard an 11-year-old explain to me that he felt God's presence as he was teaching, I did not question the Holy Spirit's work. Since then, I have continued to see Him work in the lives of thousands of children and preteens.

I have observed very shy children full of fear at one moment and then the next, they are speaking boldly like adults. I observed a young lady one evening, terrified to the point of hyperventilating. Minutes later, she walked onto the stage and preached the Gospel in the power of the Holy Spirit in front of hundreds of people.

Children's gifts have manifested before my eyes. They are administrators, teachers, prophets, shepherds, givers of mercy, helpers, encouragers, and much more. As I have watched and contemplated, they have taught me that they are the missing piece in the body of Christ. Their gifts, like adults', bring value to the Church today. Ogden shares, "Paul says that the Holy Spirit has given all believers ministry gifts, and therefore each believer is equivalent to a body part that contributes to the health of the whole." [38]

I am not the only one who has witnessed this beautiful move of God. I absolutely loved taking adults on mission trips with me. Many attended the trips thinking they were going to teach the kids. It quickly became apparent that the kids taught them. I have seen grown men brought to tears by what they have observed. They, like me, have said, "This is God moving. He has His hands all over this."

More than a few leaders have expressed shame for their lack of love and concern for the lost while watching children weep and cry for people that do not know Christ. Adults have stood back in awe as children were drawn into God's presence and then were ready and willing to embrace God's plan for the world. It is indescribable at times.

It took me a while to realize that I needed to get out of the way and allow the Lord to work. In my protectiveness, I became a stumbling block and hindrance to the Holy Spirit. However, when I learned to throw children into the deep end—out of what was comfortable—He showed up. To my amazement, I frequently watched as the Spirit took over in a child's moment of fear. Through experiences such as this, they learned even more to trust Him.

From my personal observations throughout the last 20 years, I have become aware that the Spirit of God moves more powerfully outside of my church. He certainly works in my church; however, when we aligned our kids with the Great Commission, He shows up powerfully. He is faithful to His Word. Kids experience the Lord's promise from Acts 1:8. Numerous times, children were fearful, and then the Spirit took over. Later, they were unaware of what the Spirit said through them.

This has been an amazing 20-year adventure, and I pray that you will join me on this journey. From my experience in the last 33 years of ministry, I have found that there are four key components that play a major role in being successful in discipling children: family, discipleship, ministry involvement, and missions. In all my years of working in the church, I found that I had to have these principles in place in order to have the greatest impact on the life of a child.

A. Family (Deuteronomy 6:1-8)

It has been said that if you want to know where kids are heading spiritually, you only have to take a look at their parents. Their parents—Mom and Dad—are the number one spiritual influence in their lives… not the pastor, children's pastor, youth pastor, Sunday school teacher, or other leaders in your church. It is so important that we work directly with parents to train them and support them in their role at home.

Here are some of the problems you will face with parents:

- Many parents are converts. They know Christ but have not been discipled.
- They do not understand their biblical calling (Deuteronomy 6:1-8).
- They prioritize school and activities over church and faith.
- Jesus is low on their priority list.
- They lack a Christian worldview.

We learned that taking the time to properly train parents has lasting benefits. We had to make it simple for them to start, so we helped them look at what they were doing now. What are your current priorities? What is important to you? Then we helped them understand that believers in Christ, we should look at what God's priorities are in view of His Word.

Priority number one: "You shall love the Lord your God with all your heart, with all your soul, and with all your mind. This is the first and great commandment" (Matthew 22:37). Here is what we focused on in our training:

1. Make it a priority for your child to be in the Word of God daily.
2. Be committed to helping your child develop the spiritual disciplines of prayer, Bible study, lordship, evangelism, and ministry.
3. Make the Word of God your ultimate guide for your family.
4. Pray together as a family.
5. Make church attendance and involvement a priority for your family.
6. Be a part of your church's discipleship ministry for your child.

Priority number two: From loving God, we moved them to the second of the greatest commandments. "You shall love your neighbor as yourself" (Matthew 22:39). We showed them simple ways to show love to their neighbors. We helped them become intentional in living out this verse. The goal was to help them get started in a walk with Christ that was pleasing to God.

1. Help parents discover their child's spiritual gift to use it to minister to those inside and outside the church.
2. Find creative ways to take care of the elderly.
3. Reach their friends and family members with the Gospel.
4. Focus their child on being a missionary in their school.

B. Discipleship/Mentorship (Matthew 28:19-20)

Parents have a major role in the discipleship of their children. The church can come alongside them and provide them with needed aspects of discipleship. Timothy's mother and grandmother were a great Christian influence in his life. But it took Paul to disciple and equip Timothy using his gifts to become the leader God wanted him to be.

Parents need a church that can help them take their child to the next level in their walk of faith. Be a church that provides trained leaders (Pauls) and a place for their child (Timothy) to serve and minister in the body of Christ. We did not replace Mom and Dad, but we came alongside them in fulfilling both of our callings to help them become disciple-makers.

1. We took what the children learned at home and expanded on it to help them apply it to their lives.
2. The leaders reinforced the spiritual disciplines the kids learned at home.
3. Leaders looked at children as younger saints with the goal of being role models and mentors to them.
4. Disciple group leaders helped the kids in their groups discover their spiritual gifts and use them.

Our leaders began modeling for the children by being faithful in their own walk with Christ.

- Children first observed as the leaders did everything for them (I do—you watch).
- Next, leaders were encouraged to have the kids help them in their disciple groups (I do—you help). For a season, young children are helpers to the leaders.
- Then, the leaders gave children more responsibilities (You do—I help).

- As children developed confidence, they could easily move to the next step where the leaders observed while the children carried out their tasks (You do—I watch).
- Finally, children were leading the groups (You do).

As I began to train my leaders how to disciple children using this model, that is when we saw the greatest fruit from our labors.

Channing Haye (former L.I.T.) looks back on her time as an L.I.T. fondly. She said, "It showed me the importance of being involved with a group of believers and working together for His Kingdom." She was mentored in her disciple group as a preteen and given opportunities to serve. She went on to share,

> We were able to explore our God-given talents and skills and use them to showcase His work in our lives and give Him the glory. A part of that for me was being comfortable talking with various groups of people and in front of crowds or even in smaller, more intimate groups. Serving at a young age did help me develop confidence.

Trent Guleserian (L.I.T. 2004-2005) said that L.I.T. gave him the tools to build foundational pieces of his faith at an early age. He shared,

> From daily devotional time to learning the power of prayer, L.I.T. taught me the importance of spiritual disciplines. I was also given opportunity to share my faith with kids my age. These trips evidenced the effectiveness of kids reaching other kids. Additionally, these trips showed me the importance of the local church, yet another theme that persists in my life to this day. The Lord blessed me during my time in L.I.T., and He used the program to allow my relationship with Him to grow and grow.

C. Ministry Training and Involvement (Ephesians 4:11-13)

One of the most exciting parts of ministry for me was watching children use their spiritual gifts. I personally invested a lot of time in about five preteens who grew into amazing leaders in my church. However, I realized that to do the same for the rest of the children in my ministry, I had to develop a platform for kids to serve. What I noticed very quickly was children were excited about the idea of them being able to do ministry.

To offer children opportunities to minister in the church, we had to provide training for them to be successful. We organized multiple ministry teams that trained children and equipped them to minister. These are just a few:

- **Puppets:** Children were trained how to manipulate a puppet and then present before their peers during children's church.
- **Worship:** We found it was easy for kids to learn motions to songs and then lead out in children's church.
- **Sound & Tech:** The kids who were trained to run our sound system became a huge blessing during children's church and events.
- **Drama:** Some children are natural actors, and they were able to use that gift to minister to others through skits.
- **Teaching:** Children studied, practiced, and taught during children's worship or after-school Bible clubs.
- **Administration:** Kids were allowed to take on organizational tasks and became a huge asset to our ministry.
- **Service:** There were kids who naturally wanted to help and serve behind the scenes.

There are so many other ways that children can do ministry in your church that gives them meaning and a purpose as members of the body of Christ.

D. Missions (Acts 1:8)

Once you embrace the concept that we are to be disciple-makers, it becomes evident that we must teach kids to GO. As a ministry, we were determined to have our children and preteens go out into the community by March of every year. We started discipleship and training in September, and we were intentional to be ready to go out by March. Our leaders realized that they were called to equip the saints for works of ministry and those works include reaching the world.

You will want to turn missions education into full-blown missions. When we first took our children out into our community, it was a major confidence builder. We ministered in schools and apartment complexes. For many years, we did Vacation Bible School off campus from our church. Our preteens and students took on major roles during these events. It built their confidence because they used their spiritual gifts to serve others.

To experience what it means to be missionaries, we were intentional to take preteens and students on mission trips in the state and out of state. It gave them a life-changing experience that deeply impacted their lives. We spent several months training and preparing them for the mission trip. Then on the trip, they were released under adult supervision to do everything.

Casting the Vision

Many leaders have attempted to shift this paradigm in their churches. However, if the vision is not clearly cast, it will fail very quickly. God has a vision for every ministry—your ministry. The leader/pastor must seek the Lord for a clear vision on how the Lord wants to incorporate children in their ministries. We have learned that these steps should be taken to make sure the vision is clearly cast:

1. Meet with your senior pastor and share your vision. If you are the senior pastor, you can take it to the next level.

2. Meet with staff members/elders of your church.

3. Meet with deacons

4. Meet with other church leaders.

5. Meet with families after the pastor, staff/elders, deacons, and church leaders support you.

Will You Ride the Wave?

Carilyn Tucker (L.I.T. 2008-2009) shared her experience of teaching during her college speech class. She said,

> I got up and told my story of what I did in church—how I served from a very young age in the bus ministry, on mission trips, Good News Clubs, and discipling younger children. When I got through, the professor pulled me aside and said, "Young lady, how old are you?" I told her 18 years old. She said, "And you have done all of this? This is amazing."

When Carilyn told me this story, I rejoiced in what God had done through her life.

You might have noticed by now that I am sold out for kids in the church. I truly believe that the Lord is raising up an army in our midst. We can either join Him in what He is doing or be left behind. There is constant resistance by some who just do not get it or want to believe it. They are trapped in a paradigm of the past or just do not believe that children are capable of doing great things in the power of the Holy Spirit.

Can you imagine floodwaters rising in a lake? The only thing stopping the floodwaters is the dam in the river. The waters are rising higher and higher to the point that the dam might burst and release the water. Some see that floods of revival are coming like waves of water, and it is getting higher and higher. That flood is coming through our children and students. The resistance to the rising water is the Church today and our modern philosophies. There are two sides to look at what God is doing: you will either ride the wave of revival or it will pass you by.

At the end of our 2005 mission trip, one of the leaders went back to his home church and reported what he had witnessed. He shared how God had poured out His Spirit on the kids on the trip, how he had witnessed the very thing the church was praying for—revival. Unfortunately, some of the church staff members were very skeptical and antagonistic.

The question you can ask yourself is this: "Will you embrace what the Lord is doing, or will you join those who choose not to believe what they are hearing?" You can take the road that says children are to be seen and not heard, or the road that looks at children and students as younger brothers and sisters in Christ—saints, sealed by the Holy Spirit, gifted by the Holy Spirit, and empowered by the Holy Spirit for ministry. I pray that you will join God on this incredible journey to raise up an army for our King so that every tribe, nation, and tongue might stand before the throne and the Lamb (Revelation 7:9).

The Large Empty Building

Recently, I woke up thinking about the empty building I mentioned earlier that was in my dream years ago. What did it mean when I was walking through that vast facility? Now, I believe it is the Church today. Nieuwhof shares, "What is at stake: the mission dies when the methods don't change." [39] Many churches either are stuck in the past or have lost their focus on the Great Commission. Some are resistant to change altogether.

Could it be that revival in the Church can come through our children? I believe that we need to make them a top priority and treat them as younger brothers and sisters in Christ with the attitude that we must pass the torch to what Rick Olmstead calls the "NOW generation." They are our hope and future, and they are ready to transform our world with the Good News of Christ. As Luis Bush shared, "They are anointed and appointed by God to be His instruments." [40]

We can join God in what He is doing and partner with families to raise up a generation on fire for the Lord. God's vision expands far beyond my church and the many churches I have had the privilege to work with. His vision is moving worldwide as He raises up children and students around the globe and uses them to His glory.

We Want to Help You Shift to a New Ministry Model

In 2015, I developed our Empowering The Next Generation (ETNG) training. We have had the privilege of training thousands of leaders worldwide, and we would like to invite you to join us to learn how you can embrace the younger saints in your ministry today. As I mentioned earlier, there are four keys that need to be in place to effectively disciple and equip children in your church and ministry: family, discipleship, ministry training, and missions.

Our ETNG training will help you take your ministry to a new level of discipleship with children. We will give you practical tools to get you started on this amazing journey God has for the kids in your ministry.

Freely We Have Received, Freely We Give to You

God has blessed us with a tool to disciple and equip children for ministry. We are offering our resources to you at no charge. However, you are required to go through our Empowering The Next Generation training to gain access to them.

Through the training, you will be able to shift the paradigm in your church to fully assimilate children and students. You will learn to embrace the family, discipleship, ministry involvement, and missions.

Freely we have received, freely we give...so that we can reach this generation and make disciples who make disciples. Please visit our website at www.leadersintraining.com to learn more about L.I.T., to find out future training dates, and for our online training course.

L.I.T. Was a Huge Influence in My Life by Christina Gonzalez (L.I.T. 2010-2011)

In 5th grade, I was introduced to L.I.T. It shaped my walk with Christ and taught me how to share the Gospel. L.I.T. was a place where I made friends, learned about God, and was challenged to share my faith.

On Wednesday evenings, my peers and I would learn how to share the Gospel. Our knowledge and practice would come to fruition with a mission trip in the summer. I discovered joy in service and saw God move in these mission trips. This is how I learned that miracles were real and possible.

I hold a lot of stories from L.I.T. close to me. One of them involved spiritual warfare. During a night of worship and prayer, the electricity went out. This did not stop us; we continued to pray. Specifically, we prayed for the worship leader's friend who did not know Jesus. Without warning, the electricity came back on and the worship leader received a call from his friend. We were shocked and so excited to see God's hand in our lives. Stories like these remind me of how God continues to be sovereign and a source of my strength.

I was given the opportunity to share the Gospel at a community gathering. I was so anxious about speaking in front of a large crowd, but I knew I was being called to do God's work. Before stepping on stage, I prayed with my family and L.I.T. leaders. The moment my foot touched the stage, my fear was gone. I couldn't even tell you what I spoke about—the Holy Spirit worked through me.

I know anything is possible with God and He is a God of peace. I saw this impact on my life and use it as a reminder when life is chaotic. L.I.T. was a huge influence in my life. Today, I am studying to be a nurse, and I continue to serve God. I am thankful for the foundation L.I.T. gave me to use.

ENDNOTES

1 www.4to14window.com

2 Luis Bush, *4/14 Window Global Summit*, Bangkok, Thailand, March 28, 2013.

3 www.4to14window.com

4 Warren W. Wiersbe. *Be Rich (Ephesians): Gaining the Things That Money Can't Buy* (Colorado Springs, David C. Cook: 1979), 21.

5 Wiersbe, 34.

6 Parnel Ryan attended the 2009 preteen mission trip to Kerrville, Texas.

7 Warren W. Wiersbe, *The Bible Exposition Commentary, Vol. 2* (Wheaton, IL: Victor Books, 1996), 20.

8 D. S. Dockery, *The Pauline Letters.* In D. S. Dockery (Ed.), *Holman Concise Bible Commentary* (Nashville, TN: Broadman & Holman Publishers: 1998), 558.

9 Adam Stadtmiller, *Discover Your Kid's Spiritual Gifts: A Journey Into Your Child's Identity in Christ* (Grand Rapids: Baker Publishing Group, 2012), 16.

10 Alan E. Nelson, *KidLead: Growing Great Leaders* (BookSurge Publishing, 2009), 45.

11 H. W. Hoehner, *Ephesians.* In J. F. Walvoord & R. B. Zuck (Eds.). *The Bible Knowledge Commentary: An Exposition of the Scriptures, Vol. 2* (Wheaton, IL: Victor Books, 1985), 635.

[12] Wiersbe, Vol. 2, 38.

[13] M. Anders, *Galatians-Colossians, Vol. 8* (Nashville, TN: Broadman & Holman Publishers, 1999), 152.

[14] M. R. Vincent, *Word Studies in the New Testament, Vol. 3* (New York: Charles Scribner's Sons, 1887), 390.

[15] R. R. Melick, *Philippians, Colossians, Philemon* (Nashville: Broadman & Holman Publishers, 1991), 242.

[16] Dan Brewster, *Child, Church and Mission, Revised Edition* (Compassion International, 2011), 171. http://www.europeanea.org/wp-content/uploads/2013/09/dan_brewster_childchurchmission_revised-en-web.pdf.

[17] Brewster, 171.

[18] Brewster, 170.

[19] Richard Ross and Kenneth S. Hemphill, *Parenting with Kingdom Purpose* (Nashville: B&H Publishing Group, 2005 Kindle Edition), 14.

[20] https://joshuaproject.net/resources/articles/10_40_window

[21] Henry Blackaby and Claude King, *Experiencing God: How to Live the Full Adventure of Knowing and Doing the Will of God* (Broadman & Holman, Nashville: 1994), 76.

[22] Blackaby and King, 77.

[23] Timothy S. Land and Paul David Tripp, *How People Change* (New Growth Press, Kindle Edition: 2008), 132.

[24] Stadtmiller, 22.

[25] Katherine Park attended the 2015 mission trip to Granbury, Texas.

[26] Richard J. Foster, *Celebration of Disciplines, The Path to Spiritual Growth* (New York: Harper Collins Publishers, 1978.

[27] Gallaty, Robby. *Growing Up: How to Be a Disciple Who Makes Disciples* (B&H Publishing Group, Kindle Edition), p. 13.

[28] Joel Rosenberg, *The Invested Life: Making Disciples of all Nations One Person at a Time* (New York: Zondervan, 2012), p. 35.

[29] Rosenberg, 35.

[30] Jim Putman, *Real-Life Discipleship: Building Church That Make Disciples* (United States: Navpress, 2010), 54.

[31] malphursgroup.com/state-of-the-american-church-plateaued-declining/

[32] http://advocate.jbu.edu/2019/03/06/churchgoers-lose-sight-of-the-great-commission/#:~:text=A%20study%20called%20%E2%80%9CTranslating%20the,unaware%20of%20the%20Great%20Commission.&text=The%20phrase%20'the%20Great%2Commission,the%20minds%20of%20new%20Christians

[33] www.barna.com/research/half-churchgoers-not-heard-of-great-commission/

[34] Bill Thrasher, *A Journey to Victorious Praying: Finding Discipline and Delight in Your Prayer Life* (Chicago, Moody Publishers: 2017), 3.

[35] Greg Ogden, *Transforming Discipleship: Making Disciples a Few at a Time* (Downers Grove, IL: InterVarsity Press, 2003), 25.

[36] Ogden, 26.

37 Alex and Diana Aburto, Vine and Branches Ministries, Piedras Negras, Mexico.

38 Odgen, 25.

39 careynieuwhof.com

40 Luis Bush, 4/14 Window Global Summit, Bangkok, Thailand, March 28, 2013.